Mouth and Foot Painting Artists

Text © 2005 Marc Alexander

Paintings © Association of Mouth and Foot Painting Artists

Printed in UK

ISBN 0-907159-48-6

Foreword

I have known some members of this Association for quite a long time. As a fellow artist, it's been fascinating to watch them paint with brushes held in their mouths or between their toes, and I've marvelled at the way they've overcome their adversity. But, that's really not the point... As the disabled German artist who founded the Association of Mouth and Foot Painting Artists, Erich Stegmann said, "What difference does it make *how* a picture is painted? A painter paints from the heart what the eyes see."

The joy of painting is here to see in this lovely book. Yes of course, first of all, admire these beautiful paintings created by fellow artists. Then, read the stories *behind* the pictures. They are stories of achievement, against overwhelming odds, about people whose backgrounds and disabilities may be very different. What they all share is a compelling love of art and creativity, (and a collective sense of humour!). When I meet them, laughter is never very far away.

I find this book gladdens my heart. I think it will light up your day as well.

Rolf Harris OBE AM

Rolf Harris with MFPA artists; the late Kathy Mitchell, Katrina Gardner, Tom Yendell, David Cawthorne, Steven Chambers and Alison Lapper at "The Big Draw" event in Trafalgar Square.

The Artists

PAST MASTERS

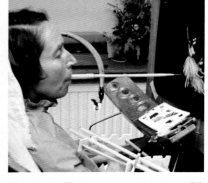

BRITISH ARTISTS

BRITISH ARTISTS *continued*

ARTISTS WORLDWIDE

Iwao Adachi p115	Eros Bonamini p118	Jolanta Borek-Unikowska p120
Shih-Feng Chen p122	Ruth Christensen p124	Dennis Francesconi p126
Kun-Shan Hsieh p145	Thomas Kahlau p147	Nancy Rae Litteral p150
Anna-Liisa Lundström p152	Serge Maudet p154	Cristóbal Moreno-Toledo p156

ARTISTS WORLDWIDE *continued*

Soon-Yi Oh   p158

Professor Manuel Parreño   p160

Elias Raftopoulos   p177

Mai Ryan   p179

Grant Sharman   p182

Phillip Swanepoel   p185

José Gerardo Uribe   p189

Introduction

Fifty years ago a unique partnership was inaugurated by Erich Stegmann whose story is told in this book. It was a partnership of artists who, like its founder, painted their pictures without the use of their hands. Initially there were sixteen members, today the partnership – known as the Association of Mouth and Foot Painting Artists – has a membership of nearly seven hundred in seventy-five countries. This book tells the stories of some of these British and overseas artists who have overcome adversity through their art.

As the result of poliomyelitis paralysing him two years after his birth in Darmstadt in 1912, Erich Stegmann lost the use of his arms, yet he succeeded in fulfilling his ambition to become a professional artist and later an art publisher. With success came the idea of founding a co-operative society of artists who were handicapped like himself.

He once explained his objective thus, 'There are people all over the world handicapped like me who have the ability to paint yet have to depend on their families or social security payments to survive. If only they could organize. With proper marketing their best work could be sold as cards and prints. Everyone would get an equal share of the proceeds and there would be scholarships for those who need to have their talents developed.

'I want to form such an organization which will work on several basic rules. Everyone who becomes a full member must have a standard of work that an independent panel of art experts considers equal to that of non-handicapped professional painters. It will be a proper commercial enterprise governed entirely by its members. It must never be thought of as a charity – its products must be sold on merit alone.'

This 'enterprise' came into being in 1956 and in March of the following year its sixteen founder members met for the first time at Liechtenstein's Wald Hotel. It was decided to establish the Association's headquarters in the Principality because of its political neutrality and the advantages of the internationally acceptable Swiss franc.

Today the Association functions on the guidelines that were agreed upon at the first meeting. It is a 'democratic co-operative', all its artists having a voice in how it is run by electing delegates to represent their interests.

According to the Association's statutes a Delegates' Convention must be held every three years, though in practice it takes place more frequently. This Convention is responsible for control of all the Association's activities and appoints the managing board that oversees the work of the few able-bodied administration and professional staff employed by the organization.

The Association is always seeking new members. Persons with artistic potential who do not have the use of their arms and paint by holding the brush in their mouth or with their feet, irrespective of age, race or creed, are eligible for consideration by the MFPA. When contact is made with such a handicapped person his or her artwork is evaluated and if it is considered sufficiently promising a scholarship is offered. Students receive stipends to assist them in furthering their talents with painting materials, tuition and specially designed equipment if necessary. This may include electric wheelchairs or vans adapted to carry them to art classes.

There are three qualifying levels: Student Member, Associate Member and Full Member. The whole point of the Association is that its members must be of a professional standard. To maintain constantly high standards, artists must attain a level of expertise that will satisfy the critical examination of a panel of art specialists before they are promoted to a higher level. Full membership is granted when a mouth or foot painter's work is judged to be equal to that of able-bodied professional artists.

Erich Stegmann was deeply aware of the disabled artist's fear that deteriorating health would put an end to his or her painting career and the income derived from it. To eliminate this anxiety he decreed that when an artist progressed from being a student to associate or full membership, the monthly income this provided was for life regardless of whether increasing disability prevented the member from producing pictures that the Association could market. As one artist recently remarked, 'What other organization would continue to keep you on the payroll when you could no longer work!'

Most of the time disabled painters work alone and understandably they can be liable to feelings of isolation. To counter this, international conventions became an important aspect of the Association's activities. At such get-togethers the work of the Association is discussed, there are workshops where experts give helpful advice to the artists as they paint, visits are arranged to famous art galleries and social functions organized. Old friendships are renewed, there is much animated conversation and an equal amount of laughter.

These meetings are held in different major cities of the world as another of Erich Stegmann's enthusiasms was travel. In his day it was difficult for those confined to wheelchairs to make long journeys, but by arranging these meetings in different countries he set out to encourage more enlightened attitudes towards the handicapped.

Among the many disabled people who have found fulfilment since Erich Stegmann made his dream become a reality half a century ago was Christy Brown. He is remembered as a writer after the success of his book "My Left Foot", but he also painted using his foot and was a member of the Association after Erich travelled to Dublin to invite him to join. Christy later described what painting can mean to a disabled person in these words, 'Painting became everything to me. By it I learned to express myself in many subtle ways. Through it I made articulate all that I saw and felt...'

Although the artists in this book are handicapped, its theme is not that of disability but success – the stories of people who have won against the odds through spirited determination and their love of painting. In other respects their backgrounds, ages, philosophies and beliefs are all different which makes them a fascinating collection of personalities. In the telling of their stories the focus is on them rather than descriptions of their work. The reproductions of their paintings speak for themselves.

For me the writing of the book has been an inspirational as well as a heart-warming experience – I believe the reader will find it equally rewarding.

Marc Alexander

Erich Stegmann
Mona Lisa (Copy from an original by
Leonardo da Vinci)

Erich Stegmann   Fishermen's Cottages, Madagascar

Erich Stegmann   Floating Market in Bangkok

Erich Stegmann   Trullie Houses and Olive Trees in Calabria, Italy

Charles Fowler Cottages on a Cliff

Charles Fowler Woodlands

PAST MASTERS

13

Bruce Peardon   The Sleepy Fisher

Bruce Peardon   By the Coast

PAST MASTERS

Marlyse Tovae   Village in Autumn

Marlyse Tovae   Lizard, *Mosaic*

Elizabeth Twistington Higgins
Ballerina

Elizabeth Twistington Higgins Ballet Scene

Past Masters

Some members of the MFPA whose enthusiasm and painting skills have done so much over the years to advance the aims and reputation of their partnership.

Erich Stegmann

'I wanted to do better than the others.'

Richard Hext had no idea that it was going to be his lucky day when he opened his eyes in his mother's humble cottage one chilly autumn day in 1956 – so far there had been a dearth of lucky days in his life. As he waited for his mother to come and help him out of bed he thought about what he was going to paint. One thing he was blessed with was a photographic memory. He could hold a scene in his mind and call it up days later when his paints and brushes were laid out in front of him and he set to work painting small landscapes. These were sold at woefully low prices to visitors to the Dartmoor village of Ashburton.

Richard, the son of a poorly paid farm labourer, had come into the world nearly six decades earlier with his limbs deformed and useless. A number of surgical operations were performed on him and though he remained unable to use his arms and hands, his legs were straightened so that he was able shuffle for short distances. While other village children could ramble at will on the moor and enjoy school games he could only sit in a chair and pass the time drawing with a pencil held in his mouth.

'As I grew older I saw that drawing offered the only chance I had of making anything of myself,' Richard once explained. 'And I was right because I won a scholarship to the Newton Abbot School of Art.'

When his course was completed he returned to his village where he started painting 'tourist' pictures, which, considering they were originals, sold at ridiculously low prices.

And so life went on until this particular day. It was mid-morning when two strangers arrived at the Hext cottage. One was below average height, his legs appeared too short for his body and his hands remained tucked neatly into his jacket pockets, but his smile was reassuring and there was a gleam of humour in his remarkably blue eyes.

'We have come to see Mr Hext,' his companion told Mrs Hext when she opened the door. 'This is Herr Erich Stegmann. As he does not speak English I have come as his interpreter.'

Once the strangers were seated inside the cottage parlour Richard listened in near disbelief while the interpreter explained, 'Herr Stegmann is seeking good artists who, like you, are unable to paint with their hands but hold their brushes with their mouths or with their toes.

'Herr Stegmann, who is a mouth painter himself, has come from Germany to meet you and would like to see some of your work.'

With motherly pride Mrs Hext brought out some of her son's pictures. While looking at them with a critical eye Erich Stegmann said through his interpreter, 'Please let me explain that this year I have founded an international co-operative of artists who, because they are isolated by disability, are unable to get fair financial return for their work. I have long believed that if such artists, whose painting must be of a professional standard, could be organized the proceeds from having their work published nationally or internationally as prints and greeting cards could be shared equally amongst them.

'Now that the project has been launched in Liechtenstein I am in quest of handicapped painters to become members. When word reached me about a mouth painter in England I came to find you.

'If you agree to join us you will receive a monthly income – an income for life regardless of whether increasing disability makes it impossible for you to continue producing work for us to publish. That is one of the most important rules. Our members must be able to concentrate on their art without feeling uneasy about the future.'

Richard could hardly believe what the interpreter was saying. It could mean that the days of near poverty for his mother and himself would be at an end and no longer would he be painting little souvenir pictures for tourists but would be painting as a true professional. When he signed the contract that Erich Stegmann had drawn up with a mouth-held pen he became the first English member of the Association of Mouth and Foot Painting Artists.

It is not exaggerating to say that Erich Stegmann, who changed the life of Richard Hext that day, was one of the most remarkable men of the 20th century. No one understood better than he the frustration, loneliness and, in many cases, the poverty of those men and women, who despite disability, struggled to express themselves through the medium of paint and canvas. He had been without the use of his hands since the age of two.

In 1912 Erich was born in Darmstadt where his father Alois Stegmann worked in a bank. Two years later the family moved to Nuremberg where at the height of summer little Erich succumbed to what was first thought to be a fever. As his condition worsened he cried in agony and the specialist who had been called in recognized the symptoms of Infantile Paralysis, known today as poliomyelitis. Since the introduction of the Salk vaccine polio has practically vanished from the western world but before that breakthrough epidemics of the crippling disease were the dread of parents with young children. After the attack had peaked Erich's distraught father and mother were told that although his legs would be stunted he would be able to walk short distances, but his upper limbs would remain immobile for the rest of his life.

Erich soon became acutely aware of his disability. He could only watch the romping of his brothers and sister; he could only sit in his chair while they played with their toys. His big ordeal came when his mother took him for his first day at school. As they arrived he was conscious of scores of eyes gazing at the ungainly way he walked and the way his useless hands were tucked into his pockets. In order to spare him as much embarrassment as possible the teacher placed him at the back of the classroom where he sat and watched his fellow pupils working with pencils and crayons in their hands.

If he felt like crying with frustration he held his tears back – his mother was not there to wipe them away. Yet as a child, a cripple among the able-bodied, Erich showed the determination that was to characterize him all his life.

One day, unable to stand his inactivity any longer, he contrived to get the end of a pencil between his teeth and then struggled to form his letters with it.

'I began to write and paint with the other children,' Erich recalled later in life. 'But I wanted to do better than the others. They wrote and painted with their hands; my hands were paralysed so I painted with my mouth. I wanted to prove to them that I could do better than those who were not handicapped. And I did it better. In fact I did so well that in 1927 I was accepted into the art school at the age of fifteen. I worked like mad and won a scholarship from the Lord Mayor of Nuremberg, where my parents now lived, to work for one year in the studio of a famous artist. The choice was left to me and I went to Erwin von Kormendy, a Hungarian painter.'

Erich's confidence increased as he became more and more proficient. By the age of twenty-two he had enough self-assurance to share a studio with his brother-in-law and set out to earn a living by painting with his mouth-held brushes. He had dreamed of the bohemian life of the artistic set and now he was able to enjoy it. In cafés frequented by artists he would discuss the stormy politics of the day and express his ideas enthusiastically – too enthusiastically as it later turned out. At this time he was attracted to a girl named Bobby Hartman who later became his wife. And, mindful of future responsibilities, he did not want to rely on an insecure livelihood dependent on selling paintings at a time when the country was beset with financial instability. Therefore he set up a publishing enterprise to produce art prints.

As an artist Erich not only painted landscapes and picturesque city scenes but pictures reflecting the plight of so many people who were poor and exploited in the chaotic Germany of the 'twenties and early 'thirties. It was a time of tension and stress; some feared the Communists and others the National Socialists. Ten years after serving a prison sentence for leading his National Socialist party members in an unsuccessful uprising against the government of the day, the failed painter Adolf Hitler became the Chancellor of Germany.

With his own hard-won independence, Erich was dedicated to the concept of individual freedom and he never hesitated to express his opposition to the Nazis. His views were reported to the authorities and a few days after Christmas 1934 he was arrested and imprisoned pending trial for sedition and the publishing of subversive material.

For an innocent able-bodied man to suddenly find himself in gaol is a traumatic experience – for Erich, without the use of his hands, it was devastating. Two things saved him during this horrific period. One was his determination – the same determination he had shown as a child – to overcome the daily ordeals of his situation, the other was the support of his family. Realizing it would be impossible for him to survive on his own, the prison authorities allowed a member of his family to visit him daily to attend to his needs.

For Erich the unkindest thing he had to endure was not being allowed to have painting materials even though he had not yet been officially convicted of a crime. If only he could have painted a few hours each day it would have provided a mental escape from the blank walls of his cell and the stale prison smell. Again and again he asked for his paints but his request was always rejected because he had used them to produce paintings of a subversive nature.

And so fifteen months passed during which Erich's health deteriorated alarmingly. Then, on his 24th birthday, he was informed that the police had dropped the case against him due to lack of evidence and he would be freed on the stipulation that if he went back to painting or publishing he would be re-arrested.

Two months later he and Bobby Hartman were married and the couple moved to a suburb of Munich where Erich believed he would be safer. He was faced with the need to make a living, especially as they were expecting a child the following year. To openly sell his paintings could mean further imprisonment so, as an old friend of his told the author, 'Erich sold his pictures under the table.' These pictures were painted clandestinely in the countryside where he was less likely to be seen by police spies. In 1944 he learned that he was about to be arrested and fled into hiding until the end of the Second World War. Years later he became an honorary member of the board of directors of an organization representing those who had been persecuted during the Nazi period, the Vereinigung der Verfolgten des Naziregimes.

It was at this time that he and Bobby, with whom he shared two children, found that their marriage was not working.

In the chaos of post-war Germany Erich sought to re-establish both his professional and private life. Some time after his divorce he married Traudi Billmeir with whom he had two more children. He returned to publishing greeting 'cards', at first producing them on thin oblongs of birch wood because card and paper were unobtainable; probably the world's first wooden postcards! And now he was free to paint as he wished and this he did with great success. In the 'fifties, exhibitions of his work were held in various capital cities.

Soon after the war Erich discovered the Adriatic island of Burano, a short boat-ride from Venice, which is noted for its traditional lace-making and colourful old-style Venetian buildings. Burano's houses with their vivid reflections trembling in the lagoon inspired many of his paintings and brought him back year after year.

While Erich had achieved success both as an artist and a publisher, he was acutely aware of the problems that beset disabled painters, especially their difficulty in making a living through artistic endeavour. Others, he knew, had the potential to become artists but were without the means to afford tuition or even buy brushes and paints.

For a long time he had been considering the possibility of establishing a partnership of artists who, like himself, painted without the use of their hands – a partnership that through proper organization could be commercially self-supporting. The idea did not remain a dream; it became a reality when he sought out a small number of disabled artists to form the nucleus of the projected organization. On 19 March 1957 sixteen disabled artists gathered for the inaugural meeting of the Association of Mouth and Foot Painting Artists in Vaduz, Liechtenstein.

'I invited you to become founder members because your work is of a standard that can be published right away,' Erich told them. 'There are others with the same problems as ourselves who have talent but need tuition to develop it. It will be the aim of the Association to seek them out and offer them scholarships so they will be provided with proper art materials and tuition. When their work reaches the standard required for full membership, they will have a guaranteed income for life even if increasing disability prevents them from painting.

'The Association will be controlled only by its members but non-handicapped people will assist in the day-to-day running of it. The job of members is to paint. Arranging exhibitions and the technical side of publishing will be taken care of by those who are not disabled. After all, none of us could hang a painting or carry a set of proofs.'

Above all Erich stressed that the last thing that he wanted was for the Association to be thought of as a charity – the greeting cards and other artwork it produced must be equal, and indeed surpass, the standard of that produced by able-bodied artists. It must be bought purely on its merit, never ever out of pity. How successful was his vision of this artistic co-operative can be measured by the fact that today the Association has more than six hundred students and members in over seventy countries.

Despite his work as President and Founder of the Association, Erich continued with his own work. He loved to experiment with every technique possible, ranging from litho work to prints made from wood blocks that he incised with mouth-held tools. And, remarkable as it may seem, he used the same method with chisels to carve wood.

Erich Stegmann achieved an independent life and the reputation of a foremost artist that had been his goal since childhood, yet as well as success he experienced tragedy – the two children of his second marriage died in road accidents five years apart. His own death occurred in 1984.

At his funeral the famous Swedish mouth painter Elof Lundberg spoke the words that echoed the feelings of MFPA members around the world. He declared, 'You, dear Erich Stegmann, have brought hope, happiness and self-confidence into our once darkened lives and have thus given us back our human dignity, the most important thing of all. You have opened a door of joy in our lives and it is our duty to continue our work in your spirit.'

That spirit is there every time a student or member of the Association that Erich founded takes a brush in his or her teeth or toes and puts paint on canvas.

Charles Fowler

'I had the quality of acceptance.'

Students at the Farnham School of Art looked with incredulity at their new still life lecturer. They had heard that his work had been exhibited at the Royal Academy, but now as he stood before them they saw his empty sleeves were tucked into his jacket pockets. How could a man without arms be an artist? Sensing their astonishment the Principal said as he introduced Charles Fowler to the class, 'Do not be nervous of Mr Fowler.' And, as smoking was not then the Eighth Deadly Sin, he added that it would be a kindness if someone would light a cigarette for him if he needed it.

This eased the situation and Charles soon had his audience more interested in his words rather than his missing limbs. Then, half way through the lecture, he announced that a smoke would be very welcome. An awed student took a cigarette from the packet he extracted from Charles's pocket, lit it and placed it between his lips. Feeling more at his ease, Charles continued to expound on still life until the cigarette had burned uncomfortably close to his mouth. With a toss of his head he flicked it neatly into a wastepaper container.

Whoosh!

The container, which was full of turpentine-soaked rags, erupted into a pillar of fire. 'It was a spectacular way of beginning a teaching career,' Charles recalled with a smile that suggested he had rather enjoyed the little drama, which passed into the folklore of the college.

Charles's easy-going attitude to life went back to his happy home life in Chelsea where he had been born. An only child, his natural cheerfulness protected him against the prejudice that was sometimes levelled at such children. He enjoyed school where his favourite subject was art and for which he received several prizes that made him consider the possibility of attending an art school. This did not eventuate, instead he became a clerk with a City linseed oil firm in Mincing Lane, commuting to work by train from Wimbledon where his parents now lived.

Charles had an inkling that he possessed a psychic streak, having experienced what he referred to as 'foretelling dreams'. Therefore he decided to be extra careful when he woke one morning, having dreamed that he saw his own body sprawled on a railway track and covered with blood. However, his journey to and from the City passed uneventfully to his relief. But on the following day he opened the door of the railway carriage too soon, slipped and fell between the platform and the still moving train. The result was that both his arms were amputated above the elbow.

'I had to stay in hospital for two months but I found it less difficult than you might imagine,' Charles once said. 'It was a great nuisance of course, but I was very young and therefore it was easier for me to adapt than if I had been twenty-five or thirty. And I was helped by the sheer sense of not worrying. I had the quality of acceptance, as indeed most disabled people have.

'I think one of the best things I ever did was to say to myself, "When I can leave hospital I'm not going to go home in a car, I'm going to walk back."' True to his promise to himself he did walk home when he was discharged.

Back with his parents, his old interest in painting reasserted itself and he began experimenting with the handle of a paintbrush held between his teeth.

'There was no other way of doing it,' he explained. 'As I said I was very adaptable then.

And compared with so many mouth and foot artists, I am extremely lucky in that I do not have a breathing problem and I can walk.'

A picture of a tulip in a vase was the subject of his first attempt, and it was not long afterwards that he painted a may tree in blossom. There was something about this picture that caught the imaginations of those who saw it, so much so that a number of friends and acquaintances asked to buy it. This interest in his work inspired Charles to set up a may tree production line in which he worked on seven paintings simultaneously. There is nothing more encouraging for a tyro artist than to receive cash for his or her paintings and it was this that decided Charles to take up art a career.

He began by taking basic lessons from a professional artist, which meant making a rail journey from Wimbledon Station. Despite the fact it had been the scene of his accident Charles made up his mind to travel alone and to this end he developed a technique for opening the doors of railway carriages with his foot.

Later it was arranged for him to be enrolled in an art school. He wondered how he would be received on his first day but it turned out to be better than he expected. When he was sent to the 'life' room everyone turned to look at him when he walked in and then looked away in embarrassment. No one spoke but the question in all minds was what was someone so handicapped doing in their classroom. Unperturbed, Charles picked up a pencil in his teeth and calmly started sketching with skill and confidence.

'After that I was ignored as an oddity and accepted as a student who could draw,' Charles said.

After four years at art school he won the Ministry of Education's Award of High Merit followed by an Exhibition Scholarship to the Royal College of Art where, after another four years, he gained his diploma. Although his work had already been exhibited in galleries ranging from the Royal Academy to the Royal Society of Painting in Watercolour, his priority was to find work that would give him a regular income.

The artist with whom he had taken his first lessons was now the head of the Farnham School of Art and, having watched Charles's development as a painter over the years, offered him a part-time post teaching still life.

Later he became an evening lecturer at the Richmond Institute. The situation was ideal because it left him time for his own painting and at the same time he discovered how much teaching meant to him. The fact that he had found his vocation in this field was proved when he was invited to become lecturer in charge of the Institute's art department and then its head, a position he held for fifteen years. During that time the number of student enrolments in his care rose from eight hundred to over two thousand.

During holiday periods Charles travelled extensively to unspoilt spots that he captured on his canvases.

'I am an Atlantic rather than a Mediterranean person,' he once explained. 'I like to feel the power of the wind and watch the movement of the sea. If there is nobody around I will paint on the spot. After all this time, I still get a little unsure when I know there are people watching me. I know it's silly but I'm not like Erich Stegmann who couldn't have cared less who was watching him.'

In 1975 Charles retired from formal teaching and planned to concentrate on his own artwork.

'You should get in touch with the Association of Mouth and Foot Painting Artists,' a friend suggested.

'Never heard of it,' Charles replied but the thought of such an organization intrigued him. He went to the Association's office in London to learn more and as a result he submitted eight watercolours. The evaluating panel was so impressed by the quality of these paintings that Charles was granted full membership immediately.

From then on his work was not only used for Christmas cards that were popular worldwide,

CHARLES FOWLER

but he also dedicated himself to helping fellow handicapped artists and promoting the work of the Association. In 1988 he was elected to the board of the Association, which meant travelling to Liechtenstein twice a year for meetings with other board members from different parts of the world. Not only was Charles an accomplished artist, but he was also a special friend to those aspiring to join the Association and those who had been accepted as students. It was not unusual for a student's telephone to ring and Charles would be on the line to ask how he or she was progressing, give encouragement and in some cases carry on a long distance game of chess.

Discussing his physical disability Charles once said, 'Although I am disabled, as far as possible I refuse to admit it and do not like the word though it is difficult to find a satisfactory alternative. Handicapped people generally are subject to a great deal of misplaced sympathy. When this sympathy and help is understanding and unobtrusive it is welcomed gratefully. When it is sentimental and sensational it is not.'

Above all Charles was an example to other members, proving what it was possible to achieve despite disability, and when he died in 1995 his legacy was one of continuing inspiration.

Bruce Peardon

'There is too much pretentiousness in the art world.'

For the first three weeks in hospital his situation did not seem too serious to young Bruce Peardon. Then came a relapse, and with it the sudden realization that he would be paralysed for the rest of his life. Each artist who appears in this book had his or her individual way of coming to terms with grievous disability. In Bruce's case he said, 'For the first quarter of an hour I was devastated when I was told that I would not get back the use of my limbs. After that I just concentrated on getting on with life. I was lucky that I was young and young people are adaptable.'

It was on a night in October 1962 that Bruce, then aged seventeen, was involved in the road accident that left him a quadriplegic. Two years earlier he had joined the Australian Navy as a junior recruit and after initial training at Perth he transferred to Flinders Naval Depot in Victoria. With a friend he went on leave and the return journey to base meant driving through the night. Bruce drove until fatigue overtook him and then his friend took the wheel while he went to sleep across the back seat. The next thing he was aware of was lying in a hospital bed. He had no recollection of his friend dozing off, the car going out of control and the crash in which his spine was injured causing his limbs to be paralysed.

It was in Melbourne's Austin Hospital that Bruce saw two fellow patients hard at work painting with brushes held in their mouths: Bill Mooney and James Meath were members of the Association of Mouth and Foot Painting Artists.

'The way they painted inspired me to do the same,' he recalled. 'I had painted for a hobby and strangely enough to paint with a brush held between my teeth, apart from the problem of biting the end off from time to time, seemed a perfectly natural way to paint from the start. We are all part of the animal kingdom and animals have a knack of adapting very quickly to changes in their condition, and so it was for me. When I could no longer use my hands I found I could write almost immediately with a pencil held between my teeth, so when it came to painting had no difficulty in using a brush this way. It was learning the correct techniques of painting that I had to concentrate on.'

A curious thing he found was that being left-handed he painted with a brush held in the left side of his mouth. And for the next two years he persevered with his 'left-handed' brush, studying perspective, composition and the effect of colours upon each other. When he felt confident enough to follow the example of his mouth painting friends he applied to the Association for a scholarship. The samples of his art that he submitted were judged to be of a standard high enough for his application to be accepted.

Soon after he was enjoying the benefits of being a student, a big change took place in Bruce's life. No matter how well a severely disabled person is cared for in hospital he or she tends to become institutionalized. Bruce and some other disabled patients wanted to prove they could live in the outside world and that by doing so it would be cheaper for the Social Services to maintain them. They acquired a house and set up their own community which, while not unique in Australia today, was a brave pioneering project in the 'sixties.

It was the lack of funds that ended the experiment but it gave Bruce a taste for independence and he had no wish to go back to an institutional life. Helped by his stipend from the Association he managed to get a house of his own where he arranged for a married couple to look after him in return for accommodation. Here he spent his time working to improve his painting, as full membership of the Association was now his aim. He found it impossible to attend ordinary art classes so he worked on a programme of self-instruction. He studied art books to analyse the techniques of the classical painters and toured galleries to familiarize himself with the work of well-known artists.

During this time he evolved his own philosophy of art, saying, 'I think there is too much pretentiousness in the art world; people think one has to be a Van Gogh, or starve to death in a garret. I believe a painter has to paint to live, and therefore I look upon myself as a commercial painter in that if I am commissioned to do a landscape or a portrait that is exactly what I have to do.'

For the Association he painted greeting cards, his favourite theme being children in amusing situations.

In 1970 Bruce achieved his goal when he was made a full member of the Association, and soon afterwards several one-man exhibitions of his work were held. It was a very good year, but what capped it was his meeting with a nurse named Christine Halliday whom he married in 1973. Four years later they were able to buy a plot of land set in delightful bushland seventeen miles south-west of Brisbane, and here they had their house built.

Bruce enthused, 'It is very conducive to painting, being surrounded by lovely trees and plenty of animal and bird life.'

The latter no doubt provided an inspiration for Bruce when he turned to authorship. "Teddy's Night Lost in the Bush" was his first children's book with lovingly painted illustrations depicting animals of the bush. In the book a teddy bear introduces young Australian readers to their wildlife heritage. Abroad it became so popular that it was translated into three languages. This was followed by another Australian outback story "Old Billy's Enchanted Valley". In this story a delightful character known as Old Billy replants trees in a valley that has been deforested and the wildlife – kangaroos, bandicoots, possums – return to it and the natural order is restored.

Bruce demonstrated his sensitivity in writing for children when, in the story, Old Billy passes away and a grandfather kangaroo speaks of death to his little grandson when he asks, 'Will you die, Grandad?'

'Yes, one day, little one, all of us die when we're old... sometimes creatures when they're young... you see, we don't really die. Our bodies may go away but all of us keep living by the memories we leave with others...'

These words could have been Bruce's epitaph after his death in 2001.

Marlyse Tovae

'I have tried to give meaning to my life.'

Marlyse Tovae was born without arms in Strasbourg in 1933. As a young child she learned to use her feet to put on her clothing, play with toys and feed herself with ease. To prepare her for school her mother invited neighbourhood children to play in their garden so that her daughter would be used to the company of able-bodied children, and they to her.

When she started school she had no difficulty with her lessons and she happily fitted in with her schoolmates.

'They were all very charming to me,' Marlyse told the author. 'Each girl wanted to be my best friend and the boys fought each other for the privilege of carrying my schoolbag.'

All went well until she was attending high school when illness interrupted her studies. While she had to stay at home her interest in painting developed using pencils and paintbrushes held between her toes. Her efforts were rewarded in the first year when she won first prize in an arts competition. Encouraged by this and in better health, she attended a private school run by the well-known artist Marthe Kiehl, and then Strasbourg's School of Fine Arts.

Word of this red-haired young woman reached the ears of Erich Stegmann and in 1957 he invited her to Vaduz in Liechtenstein for the first general meeting of the Association of Mouth and Foot Painting Artists, which he had just inaugurated. It was attended by sixteen disabled artists from eight European countries and signalled the beginning of the unique artistic co-operative that is now worldwide. The same year her achievement as a painter was recognized in France when President René Coty awarded her the silver medal of the Society for Art, Science and Literature.

During an interview in 1958 Marlyse said, 'I am happy. I was always happy. I have tried to give meaning to my life and I have succeeded. I have been painting since I was eighteen. Before that I was at a school of music. Mama wanted me to become a radio broadcaster but I love painting more than anything else. The world is so beautiful and all nature is so beautifully planned, and I am just doing my little part so that people may see this.

'I have wonderful parents. The doctors advised my mother to put me in a home but Mama did not want that. She taught me to use my foot for daily things; to take up a cup, to open a door, to eat my soup with a spoon. I never missed my arms.'

When she had her own home Marlyse turned it into a refuge for stray and injured animals. At one time there was a resident population of three dogs and five cats plus a fluctuating number being nursed back to health. The attractive ones were then found suitable homes, Marlyse explaining, 'It is easy to be kind to good-looking animals, the ugly and sick ones are better off with me.'

After becoming one of the founder members of the Association Marlyse continued her art career with unflagging enthusiasm. Landscapes, still life studies, portraits – all subjects were tackled and, having mobility, she was able to paint outdoors rather than copy from photographs.

A photograph in the Association's archives shows her seated in a field in Ireland painting Blarney Castle. Not only did she capture the castle on canvas but she also kissed the famous Blarney Stone. This triangular stone is set high in the castle wall and is difficult to reach. To kiss it the visitor has to be held by a custodian so that the upper half of his or her body is suspended over a dizzy drop. The reward for this hair-raising experience, so it is said, is the gift of beguiling speech. After meeting Marlyse one began to think there was truth in the old legends. As an artist Marlyse was never content to stand still, turning to pottery, metalwork and large brilliantly coloured mosaics, each tiny piece being set in place with her remarkably sensitive foot. Latterly she experimented with abstract painting.

Erich Stegmann knew that the success of his venture depended on the artistic efforts of the first pioneering members to produce greeting cards attractive and professional enough to get established. Thus the Association benefited from Marlyse's painting ability, and her zest for the advancement of her fellow handicapped painters.

In 1984 Erich Stegmann died and the following year board members met to decide democratically who was to take over the role of president. When the vote was taken Marlyse was elected and as the new president she declared, 'Today this organization allows more than two hundred mouth and foot painting artists from all corners of the globe to enjoy a secure existence. Only someone who is physically handicapped himself can judge what it means to be independent of state assistance and social welfare. For most of us this is everything, life itself and personal freedom.'

A decade after she had said this, the number of artists she quoted had doubled.

When she was in her early twenties Marlyse once said, 'I have tried to give meaning to my life.' Through her work with the Association she gave meaning to the lives of people who, like her, aspired to become professional artists despite the fact they could never hold a brush in the normal way.

Marlyse Tovae died in 2001 and Eros Bonamini became the third president of the Association of Mouth and Foot Painting Artists.

Elizabeth Twistington Higgins

'I was rolled away a Member of the British Empire.'

The greatest disappointment came in Elizabeth Twistington Higgins' young life when, after a three-month trial at the Sadler's Wells Ballet School, she was rejected on the grounds that she was 'physically unsuited' to become a member of the company.

Born on Guy Fawkes Night, 1923, Elizabeth was the third daughter of Jessie and Thomas Twistington Higgins, a celebrated pioneer of children's surgery at the Great Ormond Street Children's Hospital. During the First World War he proposed to Elizabeth's mother in France where she was one of Queen Alexandra's Nursing Sisters and he was a front-line surgeon.

Elizabeth had dreamed of becoming a dancer ever since a magical evening when her brother had taken her to see "Les Sylphides". Much later she wrote in her biography "Still Life": 'The graceful, white-clad figures seemed to reflect the moonlight as they dreamily moved to the music of Chopin. It was a revelation to me. Such romantic beauty stirred my soul as never before. I was absolutely overwhelmed... that night I decided to become a ballet dancer.'

Although she had been turned down by the Sadler's Wells School, Elizabeth refused to abandon her dream. She joined a dance school run by the famous Cone sisters – the Arts Educational School – and in 1945 she received her Advanced Ballet certificate. She also won the prestigious Solo Seal and then became a teacher at the school. But, while she enjoyed teaching, to perform on the stage remained her goal. When she auditioned for "The Song of Norway" she was accepted for the production, which ran for fourteen months at London's Palace Theatre.

'It was thrilling to go through the stage door and up to the dressing room,' she once told the author. 'The haunting smell of the greasepaint, the suppressed excitement: this was the life I had wanted.'

This West End show was followed by a pantomime part at the London Palladium and film and television work. Then came Ivor Novello's "King's Rhapsody" in which she danced until the musical closed several months after Novello's death in 1951.

It was at this point that Elizabeth began dancing classes for children at the Art Workers' Guild Hall in Queen Square, opposite the National Hospital for Nervous Diseases. One Saturday in 1953 her pupils were waiting in a restless line outside the hall when they saw an ambulance speed into the square. They watched as it pulled up at the hospital and someone on a stretcher was lifted out and wheeled into the emergency entrance. As time passed the children grumbled at the lateness of their teacher, not realizing then that it was Elizabeth who had been brought to the hospital.

While staying with her parents in Kent Elizabeth was taken ill and, realizing that something was seriously wrong, a local GP arranged for her to be taken to the London hospital. Then, as Elizabeth put it later, 'They whizzed me out... wheeled me along seemingly endless corridors to a room on Ward 12 where I was shoved into an iron lung and that was that.'

An iron lung is a tank-like machine in which the patient is sealed with only his or her head protruding from an airtight collar. A powerful pump alternatively increases and decreases the air pressure within the tank causing a paralysed patient's lungs to inflate and deflate.

Elizabeth was a victim of poliomyelitis, which in her day was one of the world's most feared diseases. It attacks the nerve cells that control muscle movement and causes paralysis. In her case paralysis was almost total and without the iron lung she would have died within hours. The only movement she had left was in one of her fingers.

It seemed to the nursing staff that it was particularly cruel such a disease should strike a ballet dancer, a person whose whole training and energy concentrated on the graceful movements of her body. And the ballet world was shocked by the news. In Ward 12 Elizabeth received flowers daily and once visiting was permitted fellow artistes never allowed her to feel she was forgotten. Her little dancing pupils lit candles for her in the local Roman Catholic church and in a graceful gesture Margot Fonteyn, whose marriage took place at that time, sent Elizabeth her bridal bouquet.

Meanwhile great efforts were being made to free Elizabeth from her total dependence on artificial breathing. Physiotherapists concentrated on her neck muscles to enable her to use them to consciously draw air into her lungs, a procedure known as 'frog breathing'. With this method every breath resulted as a deliberate mental command no matter what else the patient happened to be thinking about.

'It is like having two tunes running through my head simultaneously,' Elizabeth said. 'Obviously you can only frog breathe while you are awake so it's back into the "lung" for sleeping.'

When the time came for Elizabeth to move to another hospital she was transferred to the Royal National Orthopaedic Hospital in Stanmore, Middlesex. At her first hospital she had made friends with the medical and nursing staff, all of whom had admired her courage. She had been accustomed to a room of her own where she could listen to music whenever she liked and have visitors at any hour. Now the thought of being thrust into a new environment filled her with misgiving.

'At Stanmore, having been "specialled" until then, I missed the seclusion of my old room at the National,' Elizabeth said later. 'I had to get used to the new situation and looking back I realize that this toughening up process was vital to my rehabilitation but at the time I admit I felt sorry for myself. I was made to feel aware of my helplessness.

'The physiotherapists at Stanmore were most understanding about my problem and depressions, but it took many years to fully accept the fact that I was irrevocably immobilized. I had black days when I despaired of ever doing anything with my life.'

More than anything Elizabeth wanted to keep her interests alive beyond the four walls of the ward and escape the long-term effects of hospitalization. Her wish was to live at home again and it seemed this might be possible with a newly developed breathing machine that which would enable her to breathe while she slept. Made mostly of light plastic, this portable cuirass-type respirator was in effect a wearable iron lung.

In the autumn of 1955, thanks to this invention, she was taken to stay at her parents' home in Mongeham, Kent, where a room had been converted for her use. A physiotherapist and a district nurse made regular calls and when the latter, seeing her patient's body for the first time exclaimed 'The Devil's own handiwork!' Elizabeth was able to laugh.

Sadly for Elizabeth the following winter was severe and she lived in fear of storms bringing down electric cables and cutting off the power supply to her respirator's pump. On several occasions this happened at night and her mother and father had to urgently wake her and release her from the respirator so she could start frog breathing. These tense incidents made Elizabeth realize that the strain of looking after her was becoming too much for her parents and that she could no longer remain under their roof.

Because her situation did not fit her into a particular category she was transferred from hospital to hospital until she finally ended up rather incongruously in the Dover Isolation Hospital five years after she had been first taken ill.

It was in the Dover hospital that Elizabeth received painting lessons from an art teacher named Rosemary Howard. A doctor had asked Rosemary if she would give lessons to one of his quadriplegic patients who had just enough neck movement to enable her to use a mouth-held paintbrush. She agreed and her association with Elizabeth began.

'It took her nine months to master the technique of loading her brush with paint,' Rosemary recalled. 'But as she progressed I saw I was dealing with a real talent, especially when it came to her ballet pictures. As a dancer she had all the right knowledge of how a body should go. A lot of people could do pretty dancing figures but they were not real ballerinas like Elizabeth's. Obviously inside herself she was dancing with those figures.'

For Christmas 1958 Elizabeth's father used one of his daughter's paintings as a Christmas card to send to his numerous friends and professional colleagues. A London newspaper picked up the story and this led to Elizabeth's first exhibition. It took place at the Dover School of Art and further exhibitions were held in Canterbury and Folkestone. In 1961 fifty of her paintings were displayed at the Royal Festival Hall. Following this she became a subject for television's "This Is Your Life". Normally the subjects had no idea what was about to befall them but an exception was made in Elizabeth's case as it was feared the sudden shock of finding herself on the show might make her to forget to draw breath.

As a result of Elizabeth's TV appearance, sackfuls of mail arrived for her at the Dover Isolation Hospital and a few 'crank' letters suggested that she had failed to recover from polio because she 'lacked faith'.

'I have known other handicapped people who have received similar letters and have been made utterly miserable by them,' Elizabeth commented. 'In fact, accepting disability is an act of faith, not a loss of faith.'

It was after the "This Is Your Life" programme that Elizabeth was invited to join the Association of Mouth and Foot Painting Artists.

'It took me a long time to decide whether or not to join,' she admitted later. 'The contract was so good it seemed fishy. For example, I was told that I would receive my salary for life whether or not I could continue to paint! At last it began to appear I could not go wrong by joining. I did, and it marked the beginning of a more independent existence for me. Since then nearly a hundred of my paintings have been published and sales of many of them have run into millions, and I have had letters of appreciation from all over the world.'

With the security provided by a regular income from the Association Elizabeth now sought to make what had seemed an impossible dream into reality. After so long in institutions she craved to have a home and in 1969 she bought a house especially equipped for her needs in Chelmsford. Because she could only frog breathe she still had to spend her nights in an iron lung at the Broomfield Hospital, being driven back to her home each morning where she was looked after by a rota of carers – 'my human support system' she called them.

One of the most remarkable of Elizabeth's achievements was her return to ballet teaching despite the fact that she was still so paralysed that her only movement was in her neck muscles and her finger. Soon after moving to Chelmsford Joan Weston, the founder of the Chelmsford Ballet Company, asked her if she would be interested in producing a tarantella for eight girls in a forthcoming production. Despite inward misgivings Elizabeth accepted the challenge. Using music from a tape recorder, which she controlled by blowing into a special device and giving instructions from her wheelchair, Elizabeth arranged the performance, which was a great success and was to mark her return to the world of dance.

Later Joan Weston wrote in "Dance", the journal of the Imperial Society of Teachers of Dancing: 'Since I founded the Chelmsford Ballet Company in 1947 there has been nothing to compare with the advent of Elizabeth Twistington Higgins. Her extraordinary ability and dedication under extreme handicap is quite incredible. Her indomitable spirit is reflected in the triumphant sense of achievement felt by the dancers.'

In 1971 Elizabeth arranged dance sequences and sketched costumes for an experimental Eucharist in Chelmsford Cathedral. The performance was so moving that many members of the congregation were in tears while Elizabeth was inspired to continue with liturgical ballet. And so she formed her own company, the Chelmsford Dancers, who for the next eleven years performed all over the country in cathedrals, churches and hospitals.

Despite her ballet work Elizabeth put as much effort as ever in her painting and in 1977 she was taken to Buckingham Palace to receive the Order of the MBE from Her Majesty the Queen, not because of her success in coping with disability but in recognition of her skill as a painter.

'Her Majesty is very petite, being little higher than I was sitting in my wheelchair,' said Elizabeth afterwards. 'Her voice was soft and melodious, and she seemed to generate kindliness. And how well she must have done her homework. That morning nearly two hundred people came before her and only the name of the recipient was announced with no hint of what they were being honoured for. Yet she had words for everybody and when it was my turn she had a long talk about my painting. Then, by way of dismissal, she said, "I do hope this outing has not tired you too much." The page took control of the wheelchair and I was rolled away a Member of the British Empire.'

In 1980 a biography of Elizabeth appeared entitled "The Dance Goes On" which was made into an award-winning film of the same name with Rudolf Nureyev speaking the commentary. It was not only shown on British television but also around the world and is still sometimes repeated.

During the writing of the biography Elizabeth was asked, 'After all you have experienced, do you believe in an after-life?' To which she replied, 'Most certainly. I think our brief time on earth would be quite pointless if it ended in death. I am sure I shall meet again the many wonderful people I have known during my life. Without my belief in the resurrection I would be unable to choreograph liturgical dancing with any sincerity.'

Elizabeth died without pain in 1990, but on the many ballet canvases she left, her spirit of the dance goes on.

British Artists

Nearly half a century ago the first English painter joined the MFPA. Here are some of today's artists.

Leanne Beetham

'I don't think of myself as disabled.'

Leanne Beetham is a zestful, happy student who, like many young people of her age, likes to go to the cinema with friends or go on shopping expeditions at weekends. She is an ardent fan of Enrique Iglesias, the pop star son of the famous Julio, enthusiastically takes part in her favourite sport which is carriage driving and is making a career for herself as an artist. Yet when Leanne came into the world eighteen years ago it was immediately recognized that she was suffering from the disabling arthrogryposis syndrome.

The effect of this extremely rare disease meant that her muscles were without motive power, her joints were permanently stiff and she had a severe curvature of the spine. At the Great Ormond Street Hospital for Sick Children a surgeon said, 'There is lots we would like to do for her but sadly she would not come through the anaesthetic.'

Her outlook was bleak and after a month her mother could not come to terms with her daughter's disability. At this point her grandmother and grandfather, Maureen and Ken Beetham, took charge and have cared for Leanne ever since – a decision they have never regretted.

'When she was born doctors did not hold much hope for her,' says Maureen looking back to those distressing days. 'We were told, "You do realize it is a very bad muscular disease... she will never be able to use her hands or walk." It was more or less said that she would be like a vegetable. How she has proved them all wrong!'

At the Beethams' home in North Bransholm, on the outskirts of Hull, the fact that the baby had no use in her arms or legs did not hold her back. At the age of eighteen months instead of toddling she moved, perhaps raced is a better word, about the house in a small, specially adapted electric wheelchair.

'You know how children like to use their colouring books and make pictures,' Maureen says. 'I just gave her a piece of paper and a pencil. The next thing was she had the pencil in her mouth and away she went. She used to sit for hours and hours amusing herself by drawing.'

'I took to holding a pen in my mouth quite naturally,' Leanne adds. 'I did everything with my mouth because I had no use in my hands. And I started drawing before I started writing; often it is the other way round. I went to a school for the disabled from nursery to class 3, but after that I had mainstream schooling, attending the Kingswood High School and now Wilberforce College. I did not find being surrounded by able-bodied classmates at all difficult; in fact I thoroughly enjoyed it.

'The only problem I have is that I need to have physio when I stiffen up but I do not take painkillers or anything like that. Until seven years ago I used to have to wear uncomfortable splints – day splints and night splints – but then I found I could manage without them, thank goodness.

'I received my mortar-board at the Children's University, organized by Hull University, which is a six-month general education course held each Saturday. I was the only disabled person attending and I was awarded a certificate for "Achievement in Excellence". I am currently doing a course in computer studies and a two-year A-Level course in art. After that I hope to study animal behaviour because I am fascinated by animal psychology – animals are my favourite subjects for painting – and then hopefully I shall do a degree course in art. I see art as my real career.'

When Leanne was thirteen she designed a Christmas card for her school and this was featured in a local newspaper. The item was seen by Katrina Gardner, a student member of the Association of Mouth and Foot Painting Artists whose story is also told in this book, and she arranged to visit Leanne. She was impressed with the work of the disabled girl and as a result Leanne was given a boost by The MPFPA Trust Fund for the Training of Handicapped Children in the Arts. Administered by the MFPA for over thirty years the Trust, as its name suggests, benefits disabled children with artistic potential up to the age of eighteen. Jon Clayton, also mentioned in this book, was assigned to be Leanne's mentor, which is an example of how the Association's artists give practical support to each other.

Such was the progress Leanne made, that immediately after celebrating her sixteenth birthday she was awarded a scholarship.

Today, when she sits in front of her easel, she has her bright little terrier Penny for company. Leanne says, 'My favourite subjects are animals – anything to do with animals – which explains my interest in animal behaviour. I also like to do landscapes that I have photographed with my digital camera. I do not like still lifes; I prefer life that is not still. I paint in watercolours and I like doing charcoal sketches. Since becoming a student I have done several public demonstrations of mouth painting with Jon Clayton and David Cawthorne. It's great fun and it gives people an idea of the work of the MFPA and shows what is possible even if one is physically handicapped.'

Of Leanne's other interests perhaps her most unusual activity is carriage driving.

'I do it with the Evervale Riding for the Disabled Group,' she says. 'I have just finished my Grade 1 in driving. Soon I'll be starting on my Grade 2, and before long I hope to be going in for competitions. When I have a driving session the back of the cart drops down like a ramp. Then I am rolled up it in a manual wheelchair – you can't use a motorized one for this – which

is clamped into position. The reins have loops on them and these are put round my wrists. While I cannot lift my arms at all, I have a little sideways movement and I can control Pepsi (the horse) that way. I have been doing it for three years now and this year I won the "Driver of the Year" award.'

A highlight in Leanne's life came four years ago when, in company with her grandmother and a carer named Margaret, she flew to Orlando, Florida, to fulfil a long-held but seemingly impossible ambition.

'It came about through Dreams Come True, a charitable organization that provides travel for the disabled,' Leanne explains. 'Someone passed my name on to them and I was asked what I would really like to do. My answer was that above all else I wanted to swim with dolphins. So it was arranged that we should have a week in Florida, and what a week it was. Grandma shot twenty-two rolls of film as we visited Disneyland, Sea World and Discovery Cove where the dolphins live.

'There you sit in a group in the water at the edge of a pool and one after another dolphins arrive to choose people to swim with. One came up to me and gave me a kiss and so he was my partner. Of course I cannot really swim but my carer Margaret supported me in the water. The dolphin's skin felt like a cross between rubber and plastic. He seemed to be smiling all the time and somehow it felt that there was a sympathetic link between us. It was an experience I shall treasure all my life.'

When Leanne was once asked what advice she would give to someone who found themselves disabled, she replied, 'Just never give up... no pain, no gain!' This is certainly her own article of faith. Determined not to let her disability hinder her, she says, 'If you say I can't do something I'll go out of my way to prove you wrong. What I do find difficult is people who are too eager to help, who fuss around you saying, "Let me do this for you... let me do that..." and talk as though you're in a pram rather than a wheelchair. You see, I don't think of myself as disabled.'

Florence Bunn

'It's strange how obstacles give you something in life.'

It is a sad but understandable fact that many marriages do not survive the unforeseen disability of a husband or wife. The upset this can cause to an established way of life, the patience required to nurse someone who may have undergone a personality change, guilt reflecting a feeling of failure to cope, possible financial difficulties: the stress caused by such factors can bring about the breakdown of hitherto happy relationships.

However, some couples do manage to accept disability and find it brings them even closer together. Florence and Geoff Bunn are such a couple and here is their story.

Florence was born in Hartlepool in 1937 and declares that as a child she was 'very, very happy'. One of her playmates was a little boy named Geoff Bunn. Their parents, who lived in the same street, were friends before the two children had been born within a week of each other. Florence still has a photograph of her and Geoff taken together at the age of eighteen months.

'During the war my father moved the family to Blackpool because he still had memories of West Hartlepool being bombarded in the First World War when he was a young apprentice,' Geoff says. ' We used to go back for holidays and my highlight of the week was to sit on the same settee as Florence, eating fish and chips and then singing songs round the piano.'

When Florence reached the age of ten she contracted rheumatic fever.

'It was a terrible disappointment because that year I was due to take exams for a scholarship,' she says. To try for a scholarship was very important for me because our family was not well off.'

It was now that Florence showed the determination that has been a characteristic of her life. Sitting up in bed she studied an encyclopedia that her mother bought for her along with scholarship test sets. Just before the examination was to take place she was allowed to get up and although she still felt weak she was able to take part in it. The result was that, thanks to her perseverance during the illness, she won the scholarship against the odds.

Later when Florence decided to become a teacher her perseverance was called upon again. She wanted to specialize in mathematics and physics, subjects that were regarded as highly 'unusual' for girls in 1955. Attempts were made to persuade her to go in for more 'appropriate' courses. Someone of lesser spirit might have capitulated. Florence, however, refused to be deterred and finally got her way. She became a student at St Hilda's College in Durham but still she had to attend an all-male college for lectures in her preferred subjects. After qualifying she returned home to teach in a girls' secondary school.

'While I taught there I found the time to be a youth leader three nights a week and I became involved in the Church Young Fellowship as well,' she says. 'I was a lucky young woman, enjoying amateur dramatics, playing tennis and badminton, sometimes with Geoff Bunn.'

Geoff had joined the Navy around the time that Florence went to college and for ten years they were out of touch. Then, in 1965, he was invited to a wedding in Hartlepool. He says, 'I went, and found that the bridesmaid was Florence. This time there was no question of us losing contact.'

Looking back on her career at the time Florence says, 'The teaching world changed with comprehensive education. I was put in a girls' school with a mixed ability class and things were chaotic when the school went co-ed and we did not have the right textbooks. The toilets were a particular problem and I had to walk miles to get to one.'

One day Florence found her tongue and face had gone numb. When she went to the doctor he told her that it was a result of stress and that she must have absolute rest.

'I was young and enthusiastic,' Florence explains. 'I just thought my body was warning me to slow down a bit. In July 1966 Geoff and I were married. I continued teaching until my first son was born a couple of years later. Our second son was born in 1971 and I had a hint that all was not well during the pregnancy. Soon afterwards multiple sclerosis was diagnosed.

'One of the unfortunate spin-offs of early MS is that one looks drunk because of the loss of balance and whereas a helpful hand would be nice, the reality is a cold shoulder. I began to use elbow crutches but I found housework and looking after two active toddlers became more and more difficult. Yet it is strange how obstacles give you something in life. I went back to education as a home tutor and was thus able to pay for help in the house.

'Home tutors are a band of people who take on the education of youngsters who, usually through illness, have been away from school and need special help to catch up. I found I had to teach every kind of subject, and they were four happy years because I really felt I was doing something worthwhile.

'At home we began using labour-saving gadgets that in those days were almost ahead of their time. A washing machine, dishwasher, foodmixer and so on eased the problems of two small boys and my husband.'

An electric wheelchair increased Florence's mobility but sadly this advantage was not to last. With the inevitable advance of the illness she began to lose the use of her hands, which meant that she could no longer control the chair.

This setback was compounded by the arrival through the post of her green employment card from the Education Office. Her services were no longer required.

'Dear Geoff didn't tell me about it at first and when I did find out it was a psychological blow,' she said. 'I had to face up to the fact I was now unemployable. I started going to a day care centre one day a week and was very unhappy for a long time.'

One of the hardest decisions Florence and Geoff had to make was for their sons to go to boarding school.

'Geoff, who was at work all day, could not cope with me and the boys,' she said. 'I was totally paralysed by then and we did discuss the idea of me going into a home but that would have meant the boys coming home to an empty house after school. Finally we decided it would be more sensible for them to go to a school where they could live in.'

Today one son has a PhD and works at the London Science Museum while the other attended the RCA and has made a career for himself as a sculptor.

'It was nobody's fault, but I could not get used to the idea of being disabled, of not even being able to feed myself,' Florence admits. 'With nothing to do I was bored out of my mind and I kept telling myself that I had to do something, so I started writing stories and sold a number of them to magazines. I prodded the keys of a typewriter with a mouthstick but I used to lose the thread of my tale because I was unable to read the previous pages. Finally a clothes-line was stretched across the room with my pages pinned to it so that when I had written a story I could read it. But even with this help writing became too difficult.

'Eventually a young instructor at the day centre, anxious to find something to fill my time, suggested drawing by mouth. I remember how hard he searched the building for a suitable table and pencil-holder. I felt silly but he had tried so hard the least I could do was try as well.'

FLORENCE BUNN

Learning to draw and paint was another challenge for Florence, and it was one that she thoroughly enjoyed as her technique with mouth-held brushes steadily improved. When she felt she was satisfied with her new-found talent she decided to design decorative stationery, have it printed and sell it at a craft fair. At the fair a reporter from a local newspaper was impressed when he saw the display of Florence's work, and even more so when he learned how it was produced. Here was a good story and it subsequently appeared under the heading of "The Art of Florence".

When a cutting from the paper reached the Association of Mouth and Foot Painting Artists, always on the lookout for possible members, a letter was sent to Florence asking if she would care to submit samples of her work. Geoff carefully packed some of her best paintings and duly dispatched them.

When a short time had passed without a response more pictures were posted to the Association in order to prove that the first consignment had not been 'a flash in the pan'.

Florence began to find belief in herself again when the quality of the paintings had been evaluated and she received an invitation to become a student.

Looking back on that time she says, 'We think we don't want admiration yet underneath we do. What I mean is that we want to be accepted, we want someone to notice us. And the important thing about becoming a MFPA student is that you have someone backing you. And it made me realize how many fellow handicapped artists there were in the world. Today I believe there are over six hundred of us.

'I remember going down to London with Geoff to a big MFPA exhibition in the Royal Festival Hall. Seeing the paintings there I realized how much harder I needed to work. I watched other disabled artists demonstrating their skill, which inspired me because they showed just what could be done. I came away from that exhibition, and from others I have attended since, telling myself, "If I try harder I might just manage that."

'When we got back to our home in Blackpool Geoff built me an easel with a board powered by a little electric motor so that it moves up, down and sideways which gives me much more scope. I also had to find a better way of moving in front of the easel. I had begun sitting in an armchair but I could not move back to see what I had done.' The answer to this problem was an electric wheelchair controlled by the movement of Florence's chin on a specially designed steering device.

It was now Florence's aspiration to become a full member. Because of the limitation of her neck movement she could only produce small paintings at first but once she became accustomed to the motorized easel she was able to paint larger pictures. Having tried different mediums she chose to work with the opaque watercolour paint known as gouache because of its strong colours even though it is considered the hardest type of pigment to use. Her favourite subject is still life studies of flowers that Geoff picks for her in the garden of their Blackpool home. Her work has been seen around the world on greeting cards and her paintings, both on canvas and porcelain, have been displayed in numerous exhibitions in Britain and abroad.

When she is painting during the day Florence does not take her usual painkilling medication so that she remains clear-headed for her work and she declares, 'Painting takes my mind off discomfort,' she says. 'It's the best painkiller I know and there are no side effects.'

In March 1988 Florence's artistic dedication was repaid when she was made a full member of the Association. 'Becoming an MFPA member gave my life a whole new meaning,' Florence declares. 'Of course I had my off times, and I still do. If I get gloomy Geoff reminds me of the pluses in my life by bringing out something I did ages ago.

'"Can you remember doing this?" he asks. "You liked it at the time. What do you think of it now?"

'"Dreadful!" I reply, and this reminder of the progress I have made does me good.'

Thanks to the financial security that came with MFPA membership, Geoff was able to resign from his job with British Telecom in order to care for his wife full time. Talking about her work, Florence explains, 'I like to paint by myself as much as possible. Of course Geoff has to put the paints out for me but when that is done I am left alone to get on with it. I used to paint all day but as the MS has progressed I am now only able to manage to paint in the mornings.'

Likewise she has had to give up painting on porcelain, which she greatly enjoyed and at which she had been very successful.

'What I liked about ceramics was the thought that unless they got broken my work was there for ever,' she explains. 'To get the abstract effect I wanted I used to mix the paint with milk and blow it on with a straw, but gold I applied with a brush. I liked that part, it reminded me of watching my father who was an expert craftsman at the application of gold leaf.'

Musing on her life, Florence said, 'I have got old-fashioned, Quaker almost, views. We cannot possibly pay back all the good that has been done for us but we can be of help to someone else and lead lives that are productive and good. If you work hard you will have the satisfaction of knowing you have earned your rest.

'The problem with MS is that it is progressive and we have had to adapt, adapt and adapt again as my condition has worsened. No one has any idea why one is afflicted by it and as yet there is no cure. So there is always a bit of a cloud over you that it will get worse and you wonder if you will be able to take it.

'Incurable progressive conditions are a burden which can crush the spirit but a sympathetic doctor is beyond price. Research is going on all the time and I have been guided away from fashionable "cures", instead I have been given gentle sustained encouragement while the scientists get to the root of the problem.

'I have had MS for many years now but I count myself lucky that I have a husband who has stood by me. And there is my painting which is deeply personal and at the same time distinctly public. It provides me with a special viewpoint and unique experience of life which is vital to me.

'Dear Geoff is extremely calm, and funny. He often makes jokes about my disability. They are never in bad taste, they just make me laugh. When straightening my pillows he will say, "One lump or two?". I remember after a particularly nice meal we had in a hotel, having Geoff feed me in public does not deter me, I waxed philosophical and remarked that life is full of peaks and troughs. Looking at my empty plate Geoff asked if this was a peak or a trough. He wants to keep me smiling – and how I want to impress him!'

David Cawthorne

'I'm not an arty person.'

Looking back on his accident David Cawthorne says, 'It was strange; from being able to do whatever you want to doing nowt. But you just have to get on with it.' This was something he had learnt at an early age as this anecdote he tells illustrates.

'When I was a child I got my shoes very wet,' he says. 'In those days we had a coal stove with an oven and as I needed to wear the shoes to school the next day my mother put them in it to dry. Somehow they got left too long and the toes twisted out of shape. But I had to wear them because my mother could not afford another pair. The toes came away from the soles and my teacher said, "You've been using your feet as a brake for your bike." I said, "I ain't got a bike." But I had to wear those shoes for another three months before I got new ones. You just had to put up with things and get on with it, and that is what I have always tried to do.'

David was born in Castleford, West Yorkshire, in 1962. His early life was spent in conditions that belonged to what is now seen as another era.

'When we were young, our mother looked after me, my brother and my sister on her own. We lived in one of those back-to-back houses with a kitchen and larder and two bedrooms upstairs,' he says. 'We had a tin bath but the toilet was in the next street so we had to leave our house and walk to it. It wasn't all that long ago, but those houses are gone and the area has been redeveloped.

'When I was fifteen we moved to a three-bedroomed house because my two stepbrothers and my half-brother came to be with us. It was a bit cramped, to say the least.

'I went to a secondary modern school and as soon as I was sixteen I started as a trainee in mining.

When we trainees went down the mine our job was to transport materials such as girders and tin sheets to the coalface. We would get as close as we could to the face workers and then have to manhandle our load. I found mining was quite fun. There was always a laugh, no stress and you just got on with what you were told to do. And there was a good feeling between your mates. When I was eighteen I put my name down to be a trainee face worker because you earned more money that way.

'In 1981 a few of the lads I worked with got me interested in Rugby and soon I was doing all right. At the end of the season we were playing a club match when I was tackled high and my neck was broken. The next six months I spent in the Pinderfields Spinal Unit.'

This was the same unit that Jon Clayton, whose story is also told in this book, was taken to after his accident. Although they did not actually meet and become friends until some years later, David has a vague recollection of seeing him there. Little did he think that one day they would both become painters and demonstrate their skills to the public together.

Like Trevor Wells and the New Zealand artist Grant Sharman, both of whom suffered similar injuries playing Rugby, David has retained his loyalty to the game and enjoys watching his local team in action.

For five years after David was discharged from Pinderfields Hospital he was taken back by ambulance twice a week for physiotherapy and occupational therapy.

'To begin with they tried to get me using a typewriter by having my arms in slings to swing over the keyboard and pegs fixed to my fingers to hit the keys,' he said. 'It didn't really work and I found it so boring that we tried drawing instead with my arm in a sling and a pencil taped to my hand but that didn't work either. So then I tried holding a pencil in my mouth. At first I only managed to do scribbles but eventually I got control of it and this led on to painting.'

In 1983 he married Jill whom he had first met when he was seventeen, proving that a caring relationship can survive unexpected disability.

'We had been going out together before my accident,' he said. 'We're still a good team. What one of us doesn't do the other does and it's a two-way thing.'

David continued painting though he thought of it as nothing more than a pastime. Then in 1990 people organizing the 'Stepping Stones' appeal to raise money for a new spinal unit in Leeds asked if they could have some of his pictures to exhibit.

'I had to borrow them back from friends I had given them away to and when they were put on display there was an item about them in the newspaper,' he says. 'Some weeks later I received an unexpected telephone call. The caller said, "I am Florence Bunn and I am a mouth painter like yourself. I belong to the MFPA, I don't know if you've heard of us. I saw your paintings in Leeds and would you mind if I come and see you?"

'As matter of fact I had not heard of them but when Florence came she soon explained it all to me and my pictures were sent to the head office. That meant I had to paint them all again for the people who had loaned them back to me, but I didn't mind that because I was taken on as a student. In 1998 I became an associate member.'

Latterly David has given a lot of demonstrations of mouth painting on behalf of the MFPA in York and South Yorkshire. He takes a very practical view of his work and says, 'I enjoy painting whatever the subject but I find landscape the easiest. If you make a mistake it doesn't show, I mean a tree's a tree and who's to know if you get the shape a bit wrong. Detailed pictures are more challenging. Sometimes I adapt a scene by adding snow to get a Christmas card effect. I did this with a painting of a church in France.

'Jill's grandfather was killed in the D-Day landings and on each anniversary her mother goes over to Normandy to a little village there. We usually go with her and the mayor has looked after us so well that when he asked if I would do a painting of the church I did two. One I gave to the village and the other I turned into a snow scene for the MFPA.

'If it had not been for my accident I don't suppose I would have painted. At school we had art classes but I found them boring and I don't think I ever got a picture finished. I never dreamed that one day I would be a professional painter and I have been so fortunate in that respect. When things are going well I work up to three hours in the morning and do a couple more in the afternoon. Sometimes I feel that I'm getting stale so I stay away from my easel for a week and I'm much better when I start again. Now that my father-in-law has retired he often drives me about looking for places to paint, which is very helpful as I don't copy from illustrations and suchlike.'

Then, typical of his down-to-earth attitude, he adds with a grin, 'Actually I'm not an arty person. Today an unmade bed or a light going on and off is art, so I don't see myself as an artist – I'm a painter.'

DAVID CAWTHORNE

Steven Chambers

'I am surprised when the day breaks.'

The first day of May 2005 is a date that Steven Chambers will never forget. It was the day a dream became a reality and the culmination of years of hard work – it was the day he became a full member of the Association of Mouth and Foot Painting Artists.

It takes a great deal of determination to become a professional artist if one is not able to hold a paintbrush, as the stories in this book demonstrate. In Steven's case it goes right back to childhood days when his mother practised what in modern parlance is known as "tough love". It was a policy that any mother would have found hard to carry out with a disabled child, but she steeled herself...

As a baby born in 1961 Steven was found to have arthrogryposis syndrome, a rare condition the cause of which is not yet known. The effect in Steven's case was that his arms were devoid of muscles and a stiffening of the leg joints further complicated the disorder. For a while he had to remain in the Great Ormond Street Hospital for Sick Children where doctors forewarned his parents that apart from not having any use in his arms it would be unlikely that he would ever be able to walk.

While Steven's mother conceded that her son would never gain the use of his upper limbs, she refused to accept the medical assessment of his legs. When he came home from hospital she spent hours massaging his legs and making him do exercises to strengthen them.

'She used to take me into the garden and prop me up on my feet against a wall,' Steven explains. 'Then she would leave me so that I was stranded there. This used to happen every day until I got so fed up with it that I began to take steps and then actually started walking. The fact that I can walk today is due to willpower and my mum.'

Until he was sixteen Steven was in and out of hospital. When it was seen that he could walk he had to wear callipers to reinforce his legs and later his weak knee joint was operated upon in order to 'fuse' it into a permanent position so that it would bear his weight.

'When I was not in hospital I attended an ordinary school where I was never treated as though I was disabled,' he said. 'I think that this was due to the attitude my mother and father instilled in me, to always carry on as though I was not handicapped. Of course there were a lot of things I was incapable of and I had to accept that and make the best of what I could do.

'From the beginning I used my mouth to hold a pencil. I did not find it difficult because I had never known anything different. What did frustrate me was that often I could not get the effects I wanted when I tried to draw. Sometimes I would throw down the pencil in a rage but my mother would make me carry on. Once I wanted to cut some paper with scissors but it seemed impossible. "You just sit there until you work out a way to do it," my mother said and left me alone. Somehow or other I finally managed to hold one of the scissors handles in my mouth and work the blades along the paper which lay flat on the table. Since then I have always cut my own paper.'

When in hospital Steven's teachers took it in turns to visit him with school work for him so that he would not be too far behind the others when he was able to return to school. They also visited him at home to prepare him for exams when he was laid up after an accident, which was the result in his stubborn disregard of his disability. One day his friends invited him to go into the woods with them but his father forbade it because holes hidden by long grass could be a hazard. But the call of the woods overcame filial obedience and he slipped out to join his friends among the trees. Within minutes he tripped and broke his leg.

One outdoor activity that he loved – and still does – was fishing, especially night fishing with his brother at a lake near his Denham home. Together the boys would set out after supper and settle down for serious fishing around 9 o'clock. Steven used a light, well-balanced rod with a nylon mouthpiece that his father had made for him.

'As far as the fishing is concerned I can do everything except take the fish off the hook,' he says today.

Leaving school at the age of eighteen Steven had hoped to get a job operating a computer with a mouthstick at the Martin Baker Ejection Seat Company where his father was a designer.

'To my disappointment this fell through,' he says. 'Instead I went to Amersham Art College. My grandfather had been an artist but then the idea of becoming a professional painter myself never entered my head. However, my parents encouraged my artistic activities and there was a nurse who took an interest in me and my work. In 1980 she told me about the Association of Mouth and Foot Painting Artists and suggested that I should send some examples of my work to them. I took her advice and two weeks later I was offered a studentship with a regular stipend.'

From then on Steven worked hard to develop his skill and was greatly encouraged when one of his pictures was chosen for a Canadian exhibition while in Japan a rabbit character he had painted for the enjoyment of children was well received.

In 1989 Steven entered into what can only be termed a whirlwind romance with a lady named Jo who worked as a children's nanny. After six weeks they were discussing marriage.

'We talked it over one weekend and decided that this was what we both wanted,' Steven recalls. 'I went home and announced that I was going to be married and my family said, "Fine!" By Tuesday night I had made arrangements with the church, booked a hall for the reception, bought the rings and got myself a new suit. Three weeks later the wedding was a fantastic family affair.'

Despite such a hasty beginning, Steven and Jo have remained a happy couple sharing their many interests. Their four children are Kaley, Connie, Christopher and Clayton.

Steven had the satisfaction of knowing that his career was on course when in 1996 be became an associate member of the MFPA. To begin with he painted in oils but like a number of other mouth painters he found these to be difficult.

'These days I concentrate on watercolours and a technique I developed for myself using both paints and coloured pencils,' he says. 'Sometimes my art materials are laid out but after an hour they are put away again without a line being drawn. At other times the reverse is true. When the urge is upon me I cannot stop painting. I work through the night and I am surprised when the day breaks.'

Apart from work for the Association he has an interest in fantasy art, which began long ago when he was talked into working as a make-up artist. As a boy Steven's brother had been a devotee of the once addictive boys' game known as "Dungeons and Dragons". The characters involved in the complex plots had much in common with those of J. R. R. Tolkien. Today such games are designed for the computer screen but then they were played with pencil and paper, a book of incredibly complicated rules, tiny models of the characters and dice.

Such was the enthusiasm Steven's brother and his friends had for the game that as they grew older they abandoned the table top models and acted out the fantasy roles themselves in nearby woods. Members of the group took it in turns to be the Dungeon Master who organized the game while the players, dressed and equipped like the characters they wished to represent, took to the woodland to set out on their magical quests, no doubt to the astonishment of any strollers who strayed into their make-believe realm. Not only

STEVEN CHAMBERS

did they dress up as warriors, elves, dwarves and so on but they wanted to look like them. And so Steven was persuaded to become a "Dungeons and Dragons" make-up master, making up the players as the characters they wanted to be. He also designed the costumes.

Another of Steven's artistic interests was painting motifs on the bodies of vehicles, being in demand by VW Beetle enthusiasts who wanted to customize their cars. He has always been interested in cars and this extended to making exquisite miniature models. It was an extraordinary hobby for a man who could only use his mouth for such work. He assembled the Lilliputian parts, carved with a mouth-held scalpel, with his lips, then bonded them with special adhesive.

'The only thing I had to watch was that I did not swallow the tiny components,' he says.

In 1996 Steven and Jo moved to Melton Constable in Norfolk where Steven has a number of relatives. He still waxes enthusiastic about the life he and Jo have found for themselves there.

'We are only a short distance from the sea,' he says. 'In summer we often collect the children from school and spend many a happy hour on the beach. I have a cousin here who is a crab fisherman and my eldest son Christopher and I often go out with him in his boat. The peace and quiet here is marvellous. We have views of fields from our house and the Norfolk countryside is ideal from an artist's point of view.'

Along with the news of Steven's elevation to full MFPA membership came Jo's college graduation after taking a course in the care of children with learning difficulties which has enabled her to take a post at a nearby primary school. She shares Steven's diverse interests, which luckily includes his lifelong fascination with animals. His pets have ranged from a chinchilla to iguana lizards, very tame creatures although their appearance belied it. Today the family pets include three parrots, two cats, a dog, a budgerigar and Japanese Koi carp.

Another reason that Steven regards 2005 as a milestone year is that he took delivery of a car specially adapted for him to drive.

'It is something I wanted for the last twenty-seven years,' he says. 'When I went to Coventry where the vehicle was being converted to my requirements I was asked to do a test drive at the factory. When I finished the designer said, "You've been driving a long time."

'"Only in my mind," I told him. 'It just seems to come naturally. And what a wonderful feeling of independence it gives a person like me. I feel I have come a long way since my mother used to prop me up against a wall.'

Jon Clayton

'My faith was reclaimed.'

'I must admit I cried when I was told my neck was broken,' says Jon Clayton looking back on the most significant day in his life – 23 June 1978. 'I was riding my motor scooter back from lunch to work when for an instant I was aware that a lorry had jumped the lights and was coming straight at me. The next thing I knew was waking up flat on my back in hospital with heavy weights pulling my head so I could not move it.'

In the accident Jon, who was approaching his eighteenth birthday, had suffered a C4/C5 break to his neck.

'Later a doctor informed me that I would not be able to use my legs again,' he recalls. 'Well, I had seen people moving about in wheelchairs and I thought, "Perhaps that's not so bad." What I did not know then was that I would not be able to use my arms either! I had to spend the next year in Pinderfields Spinal Unit, which is part of Wakefield Hospital. The worst thing about it was not having anything to do. Before my accident I was an apprentice mechanic and I was used to being very active. At Pinderfields I went to Occupational Therapy each day just to spend time somewhere different. It was suggested that I might take up painting. A brush handle was put in my mouth and a piece of paper laid out in front of me. I doodled about, making a few messy squiggles on the paper – and that was it! I dropped the brush from my mouth in disgust and did not bother with it again.'

The boredom of Jon's days can be appreciated by the fact that for something to do he copied pieces out of books on an electric typewriter using a mouthstick to hit the keys. It seemed to be a pointless existence but there was a highlight on one occasion. He was told that he would be provided with an electric wheelchair, which he could control by the movement of his chin, but he wanted a chair that he could steer by the tiny amount of movement that had returned to one arm. There was quite an argument about this and finally Jon said, 'Give me a couple of hours in the sort of chair I want and I'll prove it by driving it from the gym to the ward.'

It was agreed and in the deserted gymnasium he struggled to master the wheelchair, which lunged in wild circles or charged at walls with alarming velocity. But after a hair-raising session Jon felt he was in control and shot out of the gym with no greater misfortune than knocking a large lump of plaster out of a wall. He rode in triumph to his ward and from then on an arm-controlled wheelchair was his.

After a year in hospital Jon returned to his parents' home at Owston Ferry in North Lincolnshire and tried to adjust to the life of a quadriplegic among the able-bodied. Reading passed the time but life was far from satisfactory until one Christmas.

'My mother bought me a "painting-by-numbers" set and I had a go,' he told me. 'It didn't turn out as it should have but it got me interested in painting. I really enjoyed it and this surprised me because at school I had absolutely no interest in art – I never even picked up a paintbrush – but now I was bitten by the bug.'

Next Jon was given a book entitled "A Talent for Living". It told the stories of various artists who, because of physical handicap, painted with brushes held between their teeth or gripped by their toes.

'That book was an inspiration – as it was intended to be,' Jon says. 'It proved to me just what could be achieved by disabled people, and from it I found out about the Association of Mouth and Foot Painting Artists. Although I had become very keen on painting by then it did not occur to me to approach the Association. I felt the standard of painting illustrated in the book was so high it was beyond my reach.

'As I got better control of the brush I attempted more advanced painting-by-numbers kits, and then went on to "Outlines" which are basically the outlines of a picture with instructions for the colours to be used.'

When he entered an art exhibition in a local village show he was encouraged by having two of his pictures put on display. He continued to work hard at his technique until 1991 when he developed a pressure sore from a faulty cushion and inexperience in dealing with this new problem led to several months at home confined to bed. He later had to be admitted to Pinderfields Hospital for treatment.

'I was very poorly and very frustrated that I could not get on with my painting,' Jon remembers. 'Sometimes I was able to get up for quarter of an hour and then I would have to go back to bed. At one point I think I was close to breaking down.'

During this difficult time Jon was helped by what he looks back upon as a religious experience.

'It is very hard to put into words,' he explains. 'As a boy I had a Roman Catholic background and later when I married I was confirmed in the Church of England. But my really deep religious conviction came when I was at my lowest ebb in hospital. I felt that I went inward and experienced what I can only describe as a wonderful feeling of spirituality. My faith was reclaimed and since then it has been a supportive factor in my life.'

In 1993 Jon met a young woman who had been a friend in their shared school days. A year later they were married and he not only became a husband but was also happy to take on the role of a father to his wife's children Richard and Amy.

'Soon afterwards I began editing the local church magazine and in a monthly publication which I read for editorial ideas I came across an article about the MFPA,' he says. 'It included the phone number so, as I had improved a lot at my painting since I read "A Talent for Living", I plucked up courage to ring the head office. I was invited to send in some samples of my work and in 1998 the MFPA accepted me as a student. As a result a whole new prospect opened up for me.

'Soon afterwards I was invited to a gathering of MFPA people at Treloar College in Hampshire. Meeting these artists and their families was a fantastic experience and when I came home I knew that my dream was to become independent and be recognized as an artist like them. Above all, becoming a student restored my confidence.

'Painting was no longer a pastime and in order to have more time at my easel I resigned from the church magazine and as secretary from the local football club. I ploughed all my efforts into painting and I still paint six hours every day. In fact that is not long enough and at the end of the day I have to tear myself away from my easel. If I am not painting I am reading books about art.'

Although Jon stopped editing the magazine to paint full-time, his allegiance to the church did not wane. When vandals threw stones through the church's stained glass window he gave a pencil drawing of a badger to be raffled, which resulted in £300 being added to the restoration fund. He is also generous with his time when it comes to giving practical demonstrations of mouth painting to further the aims of the Association and provide the public with a better understanding of disabled people.

Although Jon's marriage ended in divorce in 2000 there remains a link of friendship between him and his ex-wife.

'In 2004 I decided to sell my property in Owston Ferry,' Jon explains. 'I moved back to Bottesford near Scunthorpe, the area where I was born. I found a lovely two-bedroomed bungalow of good size and I moved in December 2004 and started to have alterations made which I found necessary for my wheelchair and so on.'

He has had a wooden cabin put in the rear of the garden with under-floor heating, warmth is an important requirement for the paralysed, and this he uses as his art studio. An advantage of having a studio outside is that when he goes out of his conservatory doors to it he has the feeling that he is 'going to work'.

'This has proved to be a very successful project and I am very happy and settled in my new home – no more moving for me,' he says. 'Being closer to town I am near to family and friends, and can enjoy evenings at the local theatre and home games at Scunthorpe United Football Club.'

In his garden studio Jon usually has several paintings in progress and, always eager to experiment, he has tried every painting medium from watercolours to pastels, from gouache to oils. The problem with the latter is the smell that is often an irritant to mouth painters who have to work with their loaded brushes close to their faces. Jon finally found the answer with the new water-based 'oils' that have the same characteristics as traditional oil paints. It usually takes him a couple of months to complete a painting with his fine brushwork.

'The wonderful thing about painting is that it is something unique to the artist,' he declares.

'No one can reproduce it exactly no matter how hard they might try. I am enjoying my art and continue to improve my development of subjects and techniques. During my years with the MFPA I have made a lot of new friends and had the opportunity to experience new things. I feel very privileged to belong to the Association and it is my life's goal to gain financial independence and have my artwork presented to many people through our cards and merchandise. Long may the Association continue to change the lives of other disabled artists by giving them the opportunity to express themselves, the chance of financial independence and, most of all, a sense of purpose and belonging.

'I am luckier than those people who have been disabled since birth and who have never walked or climbed trees or ridden bikes. I had the chance to do that, and the odd thing is that, even though I have been paralysed for over half my life, when I dream I am always physically fit and doing practical things, especially tidying up the garden.

'Do I have any regrets? Yes, I regret that I never had a chance to meet Erich Stegmann who founded the MFPA. As for everything else I believe in Fate and when there has been a bad time I have tried to tell myself that it is character building.'

JON CLAYTON

Leanne Beetham
A Small Town in France

Leanne Beetham   Donkeys in the Snow

Florence Bunn Village Pond

Florence Bunn Seagulls over the Sands

Florence Bunn
Fish amongst the Irises

Florence Bunn
Pink Cyclamen

David Cawthorne
Albert Memorial

David Cawthorne   By the Beach

BRITISH ARTISTS

David Cawthorne Country Cottage

David Cawthorne River Landscape

BRITISH ARTISTS

Evidence

15.5   In favour of any person dealing in good faith with the Association any instrument or document

Keith Jansz On the Beach

Keith Jansz Houses of Parliament

Keith Jansz   Summer Garden

Keith Jansz   Padstow Harbour

BRITISH ARTISTS

Kris Kirk On the Shore

Kris Kirk Cypriot Villa

Katrina Gardner

'I love to say, "I am an artist."'

It was called the Big Event – and it was big. One hundred and forty-four artists congregated in Trafalgar Square to make the world's largest picture in the form of a vast reproduction of 'The Hay Wain', the most famous of John Constable's paintings. Among the artists there were six from the Association of Mouth and Foot Painting Artists including Katrina Gardner.

'It was fantastic!' she says enthusiastically today. 'It was organized by the BBC and the Constable painting was divided into segments, one of which was allotted to each artist. We were given a copy of the picture so we had to measure everything out and then recreate our section on a canvas that was provided. We were allowed to do our bit in any style we wished and then our canvases were fitted together like a mosaic and the result was shown on TV in September 2004. It was marvellous to take part in it with my MFPA friends – David Cawthorne, Steve Chambers, Alison Lapper, Kathy Mitchell and Tom Yendell – and it was a fun day I shall long remember.'

Katrina was born without arms as a result of the notorious drug Thalidomide, yet it did not hold her back as a child.

'Using my feet instead of hands came quite naturally to me,' she explains. 'That was thanks to my mother. When I was a baby she would sit me in the middle of the floor and put down some pencils and a drawing book, and I took to using my toes for fingers.'

In fact she was not really aware of being handicapped until she went to school where she was surrounded by able-bodied children.

'I did not like the ordinary school,' she says. 'I used to get shoved about and pushed down on to the ground being such an easy target for that sort of thing. My mother was really worried about me so I was taken out and enrolled in a local school for the handicapped. I loved that school because every child there was disabled, to be disabled was the norm, and so I was never teased or bullied. Of course we had quarrels but we were always there for each other when necessary.'

There was one incident that hurt her deeply. With amazing lack of tact a teacher remarked that no man would ever want to marry someone like her, and that she would never have children.

'It was a cruel thing to say in a school for the disabled,' she says. 'I was fifteen, a time when you really start thinking about things like that.'

Apart from that Katrina thoroughly enjoyed the school and it was there that her artistic talent began to develop when she took up pottery and flower arranging, manipulating her materials with her toes.

When Katrina was coming to the end of her school days she had an interview with a careers officer who asked what work she would like to take up.

'I want to be an Egyptologist,' she replied.

For a moment the careers officer was silent and then said, 'I don't think that would be possible.'

'I was very disappointed,' says Katrina. 'I had dreams of discovering the mystery of the Sphinx.'

With archaeology out of the question and the secret of the Sphinx still to be unravelled, Katrina had to consider a more mundane career when she went into the outside world. She wrote dozens of letters applying for jobs but without success.

'If I mentioned Thalidomide I did not get an interview and if I didn't and just turned up they could not believe what they were seeing,' she says. 'Then I felt guilty that somehow I had deceived them by not telling them about my disability. I thought "Either way I can't win." That was some time ago, I think things have changed now.

'All I could do was go on a Government work-training scheme in which you moved around experiencing different activities. I did nursery work and learned to do layout on a magazine. When my time with the scheme was coming to an end I received a telephone call inviting me to an interview for a clerical job at a supermarket.'

By this time Katrina, then aged twenty-two, had married but she was still eager to work.

'I told myself, "I'll just be me. I'm not out to impress anyone – I'll just say what I think,"' she says. 'When the interview began I said, "I may not have had the best education but I am intelligent. When I am shown something I take it in and I know I can do the job." The manager said, "You are very confident." And I said, "I am."'

Thanks to such self-assurance she got the position and soon proved her confident words. But later, when she was pregnant with her first child, she became disheartened. At work one morning she was unwell and sensed that something dreadful was happening. She hurried to her supervisor and said, 'I think I am losing my baby.' She then rang her doctor and was told to go home immediately and wait for him. When she explained the situation to the supervisor she was told, 'You can't go now, your shift isn't finished...'

'I thought, "This is the biggest thing in my life and you are saying this to me,"' Katrina says. 'I was not being treated as a person but as a number.'

She did not finish her shift but went straight home and three days later she suffered a miscarriage in hospital.

'From now on I'm going to choose what I want to do,' she vowed to herself, and chose to have her family, Mark, Daniel, Thomas and Nicola in order of arrival. One day when she was out with all four, she met the teacher who had told her she would never marry or have children.

'She saw my kids but did not say anything and I just said "hello", but it made my day,' Katrina recalls with a note of satisfaction.

When Katrina's marriage ended she was dismayed at the thought of having to look after her family on her own.

'When the children needed bathing I had no choice but to get them all in the bath and wash them with my feet,' she says. 'Getting them to school was so exhausting that I dreaded going to bed at night because of what I knew I had to face when I woke up. Eventually I got into a routine with them and as they got older they began to help by doing more and more for themselves.'

Despite the difficulties associated with single parenthood, it was not in Katrina's nature to accept being a stay-at-home with horizons no further than the garden walls. She needed an outside interest and for the next six years she was actively involved with a cub pack, undergoing the training that qualified her as a Cub Scout leader. Finally she was asked if she would take over the pack as Akela. She was very keen to do this but understandably she needed an able-bodied helper; when no one volunteered the idea was abandoned.

At the time it was a big disappointment but today she sees it as a blessing in disguise because she joined an art class held in the village hall near her home at Sproatley in Humberside. When she took her first effort home friends asked in genuine surprise, 'Did you really do that?'

'That made me feel there must be something special about it,' Katrina says. 'It was my first attempt and because of what it led to I kept it.

KATRINA GARDNER

'Later I painted a picture of the sailing ship *Endeavour,* to give as a birthday present to my boy friend who later was to become my husband. Because I particularly liked it I hung it on my kitchen wall and when an architect came into the house I happened to say, "Do you like my painting?" He replied with the inevitable "Did you do that?" and then told me about the MFPA.

'I had seen Christmas cards painted by members of the Association but I had no idea of how to go about contacting it. My visitor told me to get in touch with Tom Yendell who, like me, was disabled as a result of Thalidomide. Tom was brilliant. He came from his home in Hampshire to see me and took away some of my paintings. These he sent to the London office from where they were forwarded to Liechtenstein for the judging panel to consider.

'That was in October 1999. As the weeks passed I heard nothing and became convinced that my work was not good enough. Then in March 2000 came the wonderful news that I had been accepted as a student and from then on I have had regular tuition.'

On 18 October 2003 Katrina married Sean Gardner, with two fellow MFPA artists, Jon Clayton and David Cawthorne, in attendance.

'We first met at a Christmas party in the office of a pharmaceutical company where Sean worked,' says Katrina. 'I had been taken there by family friends and was introduced to Sean. We talked and talked and so our friendship began.'

As an MFPA painter Katrina continues to improve her technique by attending whole-day classes at a neighbouring village. And while she is still learning, and good painters never stop learning, she is able to give encouragement to others.

'I am teaching a fellow Thalidomide to paint with his feet,' Katrina says. 'His name is David Read and he was inclined just to sit at his computer all day. His wife asked me, "Is there anything you can do with him?" I said, "I can teach him to paint." He had never considered it but he started coming to my house once a week and he started with a brush held in his toes and began to make good progress – he did not know his own capabilities. It was a case of nurturing his talent and when he had done several successful paintings I encouraged him to go to the art class which I attend.'

On top of this Katrina gives demonstrations of mouth painting to such circles as the WI and teaches at the Outward School, which is run by the St Stephen's Organization.

'It is held over holiday periods and is rather like a youth club,' she explains. 'I demonstrate for the first part of the morning and in the afternoon, the children, parents and helpers all have a go at painting. It was wonderful to see a grandma in her seventies painting with her feet.

'The sort of subjects I paint depends on my mood but landscapes are my favourite. I paint in watercolour, which I found very difficult at first, especially as I like my work to be crisp and clear. Once I have finished a painting I stand it up on a shelf when I go to bed. I get up the next morning, make a cup of tea and look at it from a distance. Then I see it in a new light and can judge what is right and wrong about it.

'I feel I have a talent but what I have to do is get it just right. When people ask me what I do I love to say, "I am an artist."'

Keith Jansz

'I love to feel my brush dance across the canvas.'

When Keith Jansz was injured in a tragic motor accident in May 1995, it was three weeks after Christopher Reeve, famous for his "Superman" film role, had sustained a broken neck in a riding mishap. At the time Keith had thought that, because of his near total paralysis, it might have been better if the actor had not survived. Now he found himself in the same situation.

'I broke my neck at level C5/C6,' he explains today. 'In Stoke Mandeville Hospital it became apparent that I would not use my hands or legs again as my condition was tetraplegia.'

Speaking about his earliest days Keith says, 'I was born in Paddington in 1961. My parents came from Sri Lanka but there must have been some Dutch blood somewhere as Jansz is a Dutch name. I got interested in art at my junior school. I remember vividly when I was between six and eight how much I loved Marvel Comics and I used to sketch the Incredible Hulk, Superman and Spiderman. Just before I left junior school at the age of ten, there were two school competitions, one for oils and one for watercolours. I won both, but my painting got no further then because I became so involved in sport... football, Rugby, tennis and gymnastics.'

Keith became one of the first students to get an O-Level in photography in Britain and after his studies were completed he worked as a trainee cameraman with the BBC. Later on he struck out on his own, establishing himself as a financial adviser and stockbroker in Aylesbury. In 1981 he attended a university freshers' ball where he met an attractive girl named Cindy. Eight years later they got married.

Keith's interest in sport never slackened and went on to include parachuting, paragliding, scuba diving and skiing. He also passed the physical tests to become a reserve for television's "Gladiator" series. Meanwhile he had not completely forgotten his early interest in art and with his usual enthusiasm produced several paintings, his favourite being a brightly coloured still life of sunflowers.

In 1995 he ran in the London Marathon and in doing so raised £800 for Barnardo's. Then, two months later, he found that as a result of his accident he was paralysed from the neck down. He spent seven months in the spinal unit of Stoke Mandeville Hospital before he was able to return home to face the reality of his situation. Being in a wheelchair he found his home was no longer fully accessible and, depending on others for his every need, he experienced long days of despair. Family and friends did all they could to help him but despite their best efforts to hearten him, he could not see a real future for himself.

'Like a lot of people in my position one is only fully aware of the changes that have taken place in one's life after leaving hospital,' Keith says. 'There was no hope for me as far as I was concerned. It was a very, very dark time. I pretty much hibernated and I was very sorry for myself.'

For Christmas that year, Keith's mother-in-law bought him the book "Painters First", which contained biographical stories of members of the Association of the Mouth and Foot Painting Artists. Keith read it from cover to cover, inspired by the experiences of artists around the world who, without the use of their hands, had overcome tremendous physical difficulties to establish careers in art. For the first time since his accident he showed a spark of interest.

'Cindy was with me through the whole thing and if it wasn't for her I would not be doing what

I am doing now,' Keith declares. 'She contacted the MFPA and through them got in touch with Trevor Wells. He spoke to her at great length and said, "Tell him to come and see me when he is ready."'

One aspect of MFPA artists is their readiness to encourage each other and potential members, and Trevor, whose story also appears in this book, was eager to give what help he could.

'Although I was still extremely negative, Trevor was an inspiration to me,' Keith recalls. 'I was amazed by his paintings and he explained about the equipment he used and the running of the MFPA. Then in September 1997 Cindy and I visited the MFPA Gallery at Selborne where I met Tom Yendell and Alison Lapper, and was encouraged to start mouth painting.'

Suitable equipment took time to be specially made but at last Keith was ready to make his first tentative attempts at painting by mouth. His early efforts were crude and he found the physical effort exhausting but he persevered and after several months he had produced six paintings, which he felt were suitable to submit to the MFPA for evaluation. The verdict was to invite him to become a student. It was his first success since his accident.

This was followed by a period of such dedicated work that Keith's painting skills improved dramatically. The only breaks he took from his easel were to visit London galleries with Cindy to gain inspiration from the great artists of the past.

An exhibition of his work was organized and to get enough pictures to show he worked seven hours a day seven days a week. As a sportsman he had pushed himself to the limit, now he was doing it as a painter. One of his paintings, entitled "Summer Drink", was chosen from several hundred to be printed as a card.

As a result of his intense effort he received the news in December 1999 that he had been made a full member of the Association. It was a wonderful way to enter the new millennium. Keith had achieved his goal in one of the fastest

times in the history of the MFPA and, as he said, he was astounded and grateful.

Since then he has gained a respected reputation as an artist with his exhibitions attracting great interest. At these he always chooses a charity to support from the sales of his paintings and prints. It is his way of 'giving something back', and he has raised considerable sums for the Spinal Injuries Association, a new MRI Scanner at Stoke Mandeville Hospital and for disabled people in Sri Lanka. He also gives talks and demonstrations to different groups, which not only explains the work of the MFPA but also gives the able-bodied a better understanding of the disabled.

As a result of his deep interest in art Keith encouraged Cindy to study Art History and when he accompanied her on a study visit to Venice city they were fascinated by the unique city. It is now a regular destination for them and when Keith paints there it has the added incentive that he is following in the footsteps of the Association's founder Erich Stegmann who made an annual painting pilgrimage to Venice and the island of Burano with its vividly painted houses reflected in its canals.

Having such a feeling for the city it is easy to understand why one of Keith's most popular paintings to date is of the Piazza San Marco. This huge canvas is filled with tourists walking across the square, relaxing in the cafes, chatting to each other and striding through the pigeons.

Apart from such scenes, Keith's preferred subjects include still life, his skill in painting sunflowers surpassing his pre-accident efforts painted with his hands. He feels that the drooping heads of these expressive flowers have their own personalities. He also enjoys the demanding discipline of the human figure, a challenge for most artists. While his pastel nudes are popular amongst collectors, he enjoys painting figures walking through busy city squares or at play on a brightly lit beach. He explains that it is the effect of the light on them and their relationship to their surroundings that he loves to convey. Indeed, light is a constant source of study and challenge as he strives to capture it 'bouncing off' buildings, people and water 'from the pinks and marzipan colours at sunrise to the oranges and reds of sunset at the end of an eventful day.'

According to Keith his art career has had the support of his old friends and, through painting, he has made a lot of new ones with whom he enjoys getting together to discuss techniques.

'I realize that I shall always be a student of art and that I must continue to experiment and stretch myself every day,' he says. 'We are all on a journey whether as a student artist or a full member and we must keep the enthusiasm to do it otherwise our work won't show the joy of painting. I love to feel my brush dance across the canvas and give back to me the sensation of movement which my body now lacks.'

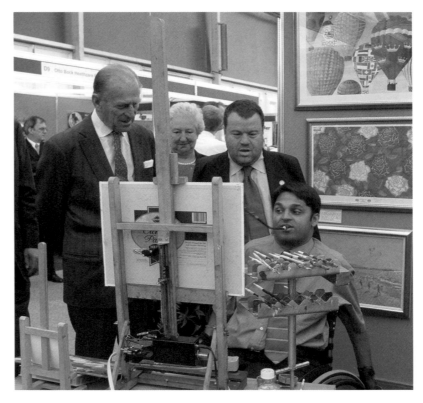

Keith Jansz demonstrates his painting technique at the Mobility Roadshow while HRH The Duke of Edinburgh and Tom Yendell look on.

KEITH JANSZ

Kris Kirk

'I like to think there is some magic in the world.'

Night had fallen on the Cypriot village of Lio Petri when there was a knock on the door of the house that Kyriacos Kyriacou, better known as an artist by his anglicized name Kris Kirk, shared with his parents. When the door was opened he saw from his wheelchair a beautiful Asian girl standing beside her suitcase on the threshold.

'My name is Blandia, Blandia Sorita, and I have just arrived from the Philippines,' she announced. 'I am a haemo-biological nurse and I signed up with an agency to work in a hospital. I was given this address but this is a house, it is not a hospital. There must be a mistake.'

'My parents had been looking after me ever since my accident,' Kris explains. 'I felt the point had come for them to have more time for themselves so I applied to an agency for a carer. Obviously there had been a mix up at the agency so that instead of doing highly specialized work in a hospital Blandia was sent to look after me. I felt really bad about it and told her that because of the mix-up she was under no obligation to me. She laughed and said, "In that case I'll give it a go! God must have sent me here. I came to Cyprus to work for a year and then I am going to America."'

Blandia not only settled in Kris's home but also into village life where her happy disposition soon endeared her to the locals.

Kris was born in England in 1956, his parents having come to London from Cyprus. As a boy, sport became his passion. At the Christopher Wren School in Southall he not only captained the school's cricket and baseball teams but also was captain of the First XV. As a junior Rugby player he represented London, Middlesex and South East England. Meanwhile his father and mother maintained the Greek Cypriot tradition of 'family togetherness', something that was to be a vitally important factor in Kris's life, and frequent family functions ensured that relatives kept in touch.

One weekend in 1973 there was such an outing to Brighton. On the seashore Kris and his cousin saw young men diving into the sea from a groyne. The boys could not resist the challenge and joined in.

After several successful dives Kris decided to have just one more before he returned to the beach party. Then, as he plunged below the surface, something went wrong. He was aware of a painful impact as his head struck the sandy bottom at an awkward angle.

'When I came to the surface I opened my eyes and found I could not move,' he recalls. 'My body refused to obey me and I just floated. Realizing there was something wrong my cousin dived in after me and pulled me out of the water. On the beach the family gathered round but I still could not move. An ambulance came and I was rushed to Brighton Hospital.' Here his paralysis was diagnosed as being due to a broken neck. He was put into traction and two days later admitted to Stoke Mandeville Hospital. He was to remain there for a year during which physiotherapists did everything in their power to restore his muscular control but finally they had to accept that it was impossible for him to regain the use of his hands.

In an attempt to revive his ability to write it was suggested that, as Kris retained some head movement, the simplest method would be for him to use a pencil held between his teeth.

'They thought it would be useful if I could sign my name and even write letters,' he explains. 'At that time, even though I had taken an

O-Level in art, it did not occur to me that there was any future for me as an artist. But once, when I was not busy practising my letters, I did try a drawing.

'One of my early attempts was supposed to be a lion, but as to how good it was I can only say that when my doctor came on his rounds and saw it he quoted, "Tyger, Tyger, burning bright..."'

When Kris finally left hospital schoolteachers came to his home to set him lessons. One of these visiting tutors was an art specialist and, seeing the progress Kris had made in manipulating a mouth-held pencil, arranged for him to be taken to college once a week to see if he could manage an art course. The experiment worked well and Kris earned an A-Level, which led to a Government-backed body named Rehab arranging for an art teacher to visit him.

When the period with Rehab came to an end it meant that officially his studies were over. Being a young man of independent spirit, he set about getting regular employment and applied for a number of jobs that might be suitable for a disabled person. In every case he was accepted but to his deep disappointment he could not take any of them up. Without his own means of transport, getting to and from a city office was too difficult.

'I realized sadly that I could only work at home but there was not much opportunity for that,' Kris says. 'Then in 1978 I remembered that a physiotherapist had once told me about an organization for disabled artists who, unable to paint with their hands, painted by mouth or foot. At the time it did not occur to me that I might be suitable but now I got in touch with them.'

Kris was visited by the mouth painting artist Charles Fowler whose story is also told in this book. As a senior member of the MFPA, he took an enthusiastic interest in handicapped people whose artistic potential might qualify them for the Association's student scheme.

'He looked through all my work and chose four pictures to take away for the Association to evaluate,' Kris says. 'That Christmas I had the best present I have ever received. Word came that the Association was willing to take me on as a student!'

To be accepted as a full member by the MFPA now became the most important goal in Kris's life. By 10 o'clock each morning Kris, having been dressed and given his breakfast, took a brush handle or a pencil between his teeth and set to work. His only break during the day was the half hour when he was fed his lunch, and he did not finish until around 7 o'clock when sheer exhaustion forced him to give up.

It became a point of honour to send sixteen paintings to the MFPA every three months. In 1982 his determination was rewarded when he was notified that from then on he was a full member of the Association.

'It was the best thing that had happened to me since my accident,' Kris declares today. 'Apart from anything else I found the MFPA to be most understanding. To give you an example, as a result of being incapacitated I am troubled with recurring kidney infection. When this happens it is impossible for me to paint yet I am not made to feel that I am letting the Association down.'

As a boy Kris had always been fascinated by his parents' reminiscences of Cyprus, and it had been a childhood dream to visit the island of his forefathers. When he became a professional artist that dream became a possibility. Thus a year after joining the MFPA he was able to travel to Cyprus in the care of his parents. The Mediterranean scenery inspired the artist in Kris but above all it was the warmth of the welcome he received from his relatives whom he had never met before that overwhelmed him.

Looking back on that first visit Kris says, 'It was great. It was upsetting. It was everything you could want. It was the experience of a lifetime! For me the island was like paradise.' Under its spell he attempted to paint out of doors but found this to be difficult because of the heat. This did not seem to trouble some monks he met when he visited their monastery and saw a number of them painting icons in the hot sun despite their heavy black robes. He was fascinated to watch their technique but his visit was short-lived. On a slope below the monastery were a number of beehives and, according to Kris, 'great big monstrous bees buzzed round and frightened the living daylights out of me'.

The situation might have had its humorous side until one remembers that for those paralysed like Kris it is impossible to brush away an insect. Indeed the nuisance of insects is one of the great drawbacks for MFPA members who want to paint outdoors. In 1990 Kris and his parents returned to Cyprus to live permanently in the village of Lio Petri where Kris's father had been born.

'It is one of the "red villages",' Kris explains. 'The name comes from the reddish colour of the earth there. It is close to a beautiful fishing harbour, which is ideal for me because I love to paint boats. I seem to have fitted into village life very well. Here one is never short of company, especially as schools in Cyprus close early in the afternoon and my relatives' children flock to the house. In the evenings there are often visitors who come to gossip and play cards, especially a game called "Spades", which I don't think is played in England. Life in Lio Petri is slow and comfortable, and ideal for a painter with its wonderfully clear light.'

Working in oils, Kris uses very short handled brushes, which give him greater control of the paint than normal ones. However, this presents a problem as, having to work so close to the canvas, it is a strain on his eyesight.

Describing his technique, Kris says, 'I put my paintings straight on to the canvas after drawing the outlines in paint – not pencil – and in my mind I know exactly what I want to do. Then I can do the painting straight off on the canvas.'

Not all of his pictures are produced for cards and prints and for showing at exhibitions. Some are 'just for himself', surreal works that mirror a fantastical side of his imagination. This inspiration has developed as a substitute for physical activity so he can create his own world with paint, which gives him the sensation of being free from disability.

When discussing his disability he says, 'What I still regret is not being able to take part in sport. For me Rugby was not just a game, it was a way of life at the Christopher Wren School. So I find it's best not to dwell on the past and I try to concentrate on the things that I am good at today and keep them to the forefront. But I must admit there have been times when I thought God had been unfair, but then how can one expect life to be perfect?

'When you look into the infinity of space it certainly gets things into perspective. And with so many hundreds of galaxies in the universe I like to think that everyone has their own particular star. I also like to think there is some magic in the world, that unicorns once existed... I love the idea of unicorns.'

Kris's belief in the magical side of life was reinforced when Blandia Sorita arrived at his house by accident and decided to look after him until she went to America.

'She turned out to be a wonderful carer and we became great friends,' Kris says. 'As time passed we grew closer and when the first year ended she did not leave for America. Then two-and-a-half years after she had arrived in Lio Petri something happened that was like a bolt from the blue – we got married.

'I had believed I would never ever get married and I was getting rather set in my ways, then suddenly I had a new life to look forward to. Blandia is an amazing person. She has such a happy personality and after my brushes have been put away the highlight of my day is when we sit quietly together to watch the marvellous sunsets that we have here and our world is at peace.

'If I was told I could alter my life I do not think I would change a single minute otherwise I would never have experienced the closeness I have enjoyed with my parents, I would never have become an artist and Blandia would not have come into my life. I am a very happy man.'

Sandy Kozikowska

'When I am painting I forget about pain.'

Orbost House, one of the most impressive houses on the Isle of Skye, is situated in what might be called MacLeod Country. Close by is Dunvegan Castle, home of the 29th Chief of the MacLeod Clan, where the clan's magical "Fairy Flag" is on display. From the windows of Orbost House guests can look across a vast lawn to the waters of Loch Dunvegan and appreciate the rugged scenery and the remarkable northern light that has lured many painters to that region.

The house not only provides accommodation for visitors but is also the home of Sandy Kozikowska and her family. Overcoming the handicap of an unexpected disability, she is making a name for herself among the artists who find the island an inspiring place for their work. She tells her story simply even though it is a story of a dream that was shattered when it was about to come true, and which still came true in the end.

'I had an idyllic childhood in South Africa,' Sandy says. 'At school I did athletics and competitive swimming, and all games – hockey, basketball, squash, tennis, netball. At that stage I was unaware of how privileged we were and as children we were isolated from the politics that were going on in the country. We had a lovely home and most of my early life was spent out of doors.'

Sandy was born in a small town named Springs in the Transvaal in 1950. Her father's side of the family had emigrated from Ireland at the time of the potato famine, on her mother's side there was a mixture of Scottish and Russian blood. Her father had been a pilot in the South African Air Force and had his own flying school, but when Sandy was five years old the family moved to Pietermaritzburg where he became the city engineer.

As a girl she enjoyed drawing and painting and was very keen to take art at school but was warned how difficult it would be to make a living at it even as a commercial artist. 'You would never get a job,' she was told so that idea was abandoned and subsequently she trained as a medical laboratory scientist and worked in a haematology and blood transfusion laboratory.

'Today I love painting flowers,' she explains. 'I think that goes back to when we went on camping holidays to the mountains. The countryside of South Africa was inspiring with its beautiful wild flowers. I remember that there were the most wonderful pink and white flowers called cosmos, some of which I used to bring home to draw.'

Sandy had always been a camping enthusiast and when she was twenty-two she left home for a six-week camping tour of Europe. This led to a decision to remain in England and stay with a cousin who lived in London. She set about getting a job but her South African qualifications were not recognized in this country. Undeterred, she obtained a work permit, found part-time work in a hospital and went back to college in order to gain British qualifications. At this time she met her future husband, George Kozikowska, the son of Polish parents, who was studying microbiology.

'We used to spend as much time as we could camping in the Scottish highlands and on Mull and Iona,' Sandy says. Iona with its peaceful aura became so special to them that in 1976 they were married there in St Oran's chapel, which was built during the lifetime of St Colomba.

After the wedding the couple settled in London with George working in Harley Street and Sandy employed in a hospital laboratory. Apart from his regular work George's special interest was archaeology. He had qualified in the subject when a student by taking evening courses on top of his regular studies.

When their daughter Katyana was followed by their son Alex, the couple began to feel dissatisfied with their life in London. They still felt the lure of Scotland and believed that the countryside there would be better for the children than a city environment. The Isle of Skye seemed to be the ideal place and they began saving hard towards this goal.

'We were looking for a small place to live but we realized that we would have to find a way of making a living,' says Sandy. 'Some people think that it is wonderful to come to Skye but there are not a lot of work opportunities.'

As there were no openings for people with Sandy's and George's qualifications they decided they would buy a suitable house and run it as a holiday establishment. Eagerly they scanned the property pages in newspapers until one day in 1990 George telephoned Sandy from work.

'He told me that he had seen an ad for a place that was just what we had in mind,' says Sandy. 'So we got in the car with the kids and came up here to see it. On arrival we were disappointed to find too many people were interested in it and as it would go to the highest bidder under the Scottish system our chances were small.

'Just before returning to London we went into Portree where we and found an estate agent's office. Though it was closed the agent opened up good-naturedly and when we told him what we were after he said, "I know just the place and it's not yet on the market." He took us to Orbost House, which seemed so imposing with its stone walls. After we had looked around it for just twenty minutes we knew it was for us. It seemed to welcome us and it was so big that we would be able to convert part of it into two self-service flats for tourists and also offer dinner, bed and breakfast.

To Sandy and George, Orbost House was a dream come true and they set to work to get it ready for business. Early one January morning

they set off for Inverness to buy furniture for the self-service flats. Katyana and Alex and a friend sat in the back of the car with Sandy in the front seat.

'There was a light covering of snow on the road,' says Sandy. 'I remember saying to George "Look at the deer" because they were coming down from the hills and were so beautiful. The next minute the car skidded and slid into the path of an oncoming coal lorry, and that was it really.

'I was the only one badly hurt in the crash and I was taken by helicopter to hospital in Inverness. It was there that I realized I had lost the feeling in my hands.

'It was decided to air-lift me to the Spinal Injuries Unit in Musselburgh where I was to stay for ten months while the children were in London being looked after by George's parents. In fact there had been a C5/C6 break in my spine, a complete break, but nobody told me that. I found out the truth by degrees.

'Now I cannot remember the pain but I do remember the shock of realizing that I was paralysed, but that was fifteen years ago and I say to myself, "This is the way you are now – you must make the most of it."'

When Sandy returned to Orbost House it seemed that the dream of an independent life in Skye was shattered but together the couple set about putting the pieces of the dream together again. Although people said that she and George would not be able to manage, alterations were made to accommodate her and her wheelchair. Work went ahead to complete the holiday flats and let them, as they are today.

During sessions of occupational therapy in the spinal unit Sandy began learning to write with a pencil held between her teeth.

'I had been interested in painting but I did not think of trying it with my mouth,' Sandy explains. 'Then one day I just started and after that I more or less taught myself the technique. At the Resource Centre, the only wheelchair accessible building in Skye, there was an artist named Ruth who started teaching me there once a week. I found it easier when the handles of my paintbrushes were made longer and I got a lot of satisfaction out of it. At last this was something I could do on my own!

'Later on a friend named Diana came up here to set herself up as an artist and she gave me lessons and became my main inspiration. Three years ago she said, "You should submit some of your paintings to the Association of Mouth and Foot Painting Artists." We chose six, sent them off and I didn't think anything more about it until to my delight I was informed that I had been accepted as a student. I still go to Diana's studio for a whole day's painting once a week where I really work hard to improve my skill.'

Sandy found that apart from the help given to her as a student, there was another great advantage in belonging to the MFPA. This was when she went to the annual week-long meeting of MFPA artists at Treloar College.

'Up here in Skye I am obviously isolated from artists in my position,' Sandy says. 'So it was inspiring to meet fellow disabled painters, make friends, attend seminars and special painting sessions held by experts.'

While Sandy concentrates on her work, George spends his free time immersed in his old love of archaeology. He and several fellow archaeologists are involved in the exciting excavation of a cave on the island where two-and-a-half thousand years ago an unknown people left relics of their daily lives and stone artefacts which have remained undisturbed until now.

When Sandy was a girl she drew wild flowers that she picked in the hills. Today her love of flowers as a subject continues in studies of blooms in which light seems to shine through petals, which have the most delicate colour tones. Although she began painting with oils she turned to watercolours to get more translucent effects.

'Since I began the scholarship I focus on the requirements of the MFPA,' Sandy says. 'Apart from my flower pictures I am working on children's cards based on a couple of teddy bears.'

She adds a remark similar to those expressed by some other artists in this book, 'I still get a lot of discomfort but I forget about pain when I am painting.'

SANDY KOZIKOWSKA

Alison Lapper

'The MFPA has been my springboard.'

In Trafalgar Square stand three royal bronze statues; Charles I, James II and George IV – and a 16ft white marble figure of a woman, naked, disabled and visibly expecting a child. It is entitled "Alison Lapper Pregnant" and the story behind it is as remarkable as the fact that such a statue should be placed in this hallowed site. It goes back to when Alison Lapper was born in Burton-on-Trent in 1965.

'After my birth my mother did not even see me,' Alison recalls. 'Because I was disabled she was told that if I survived I would never be more than a "stuffed cabbage in a wheelchair". The system took me away from my mother and placed me in an institution.'

The disability, which was the cause of the baby being taken away immediately after her birth, was due to a condition known as phocomelia. It meant that Alison came into the world with no arms and shortened legs so that she has frequently been taken to be a victim of Thalidomide. 'But I'm just a natural abnormality,' she says with her typical brand of humour.

The institution to which she was taken was Chailey Heritage, which was to be her home for the next seventeen years.

'Part hospital, part school, it was a little world of its own,' she says. 'At first I was in the hospital section looked after by nurses and as I grew older I progressed through different wards, and there were a lot of experiments done with artificial limbs. At times we were like guinea-pigs. They tried fitting us with gas-powered prosthetic limbs but as we grew they had to use bigger and bigger gas cylinders until we looked like Daleks. So that experiment was dropped.

'At the age of four my mother returned into my life and I was able to stay with her during school holidays but my real home was Chailey. It was really good for someone like me, the staff pushed you the whole time. The message was always. "You must be independent. You must do it on your own."

'It may sound odd but I did not believe I was disabled until I was twelve – can you believe that! The realization came when I went to a "normal" youth club. It was a terrible shock. It was a crucial time in my life. I had just had a major operation; they took out my ankle bone and turned my foot right round. While this was going on I was starting to get interested in boys and I did not know what to do with myself. I felt I was going backwards rather than forward. It took me until I was in my twenties to come to terms with my disability.

'Chailey was my life, and I used to think "What am I going to do when I leave here?" When the time came to go I was so petrified at the thought of leaving I refused to budge. It took four people to put me on the coach.'

From Chailey Alison was taken to Banstead Place Residential Centre in Surrey. Here, to get her accustomed to life in the outside world, she would be sent to the nearby village to collect her money, go shopping and look after herself. At first everything seemed new and unfamiliar, she did not even know what a cheque was. The process of integration was continued with Alison, wearing artificial legs, attending a normal college.

To begin with Alison had used her foot to hold a pencil but after an operation on her foot she began using a mouthstick and at the new school she enjoyed drawing by this method. Her first efforts, while still a teenager, were little matchstick figures which, in comic strip form, played out stories from her imagination, usually tales of tragic love affairs. Around the time she passed her CSEs she entered a school painting competition with the first prize being a trip to Lourdes. By now she had progressed from her stick people to proper painting and her picture based on one of the Stations of the Cross secured her the first prize. A newspaper carried a story on her which was seen by the MFPA, and this led to her being awarded a scholarship.

When Alison reached the age of nineteen she decided that she wanted to go to London to further her interest in art. Banstead agreed and arranged for her to have a room in a hostel in Baron's Court from where she attended the West London College to study for an A-Level in art.

'I failed miserably but in other ways college was a success,' she said. 'It made me force myself to get over my fear of people. The college was massive, and rather rough, and I found everything hard because I felt there was something incredibly wrong about me. I used to wear my artificial legs to try and look normal. Then, as I got older, I thought, "Who am I trying to kid? I don't need to have arms and legs if I can come across as a reasonable human being."

'I felt a great sense of achievement when I decided to do this and get about on the legs I had. I believed the more people who meet me as I am the more people will be comfortable with disabled persons. When someone makes a mistake and goes to shake hands with me or hand me a cup of tea, it is not embarrassing but the biggest compliment I can have because they forget I am disabled and just see me as Alison.'

As time passed the MFPA became increasingly important in Alison's life. When she finished her college course, aged twenty three, arrangements were made for her to attend the Heatherly School of Fine Art situated off New King's Road in Chelsea. By now she was happily living alone in a ground floor flat in a quiet street in Shepherd's Bush and used a specially adapted Mini Metro to get to her classes.

'I was nineteen when I learned to drive using my shoulder to steer with a joystick,' she said.

'When I passed my driving test it was like being given wings.'

Thanks to the quality of the portfolio of artwork she built up while at the Heatherly School Alison was accepted by the University of Brighton. Here she subsequently gained a first-class honours degree in fine art.

In discussing her work she explains, 'When it comes to materials I have tried everything. I nearly poisoned myself with oils, now I use acrylic. But I believe texture is equally as important as the colours you use and I have painted on anything that I can get hold of that has an interesting surface. A lot of my work is experimental. I am always trying something different. I am fascinated by the possibilities of photography.

'My paintings are scenes that are suitable for greeting cards and about people reflecting how I integrate with them, how other people affect me, how I affect them and how I feel about life deep down. I love to paint beautiful bodies. You might think it is some sort of wishful thinking, that I am portraying how I think I ought to be but it's not a negative thing. It is not me saying, "This is how I wish I was." This is me saying, "I look at your body and find it beautiful." To capture the beauty of the human body is what I strive for all the time. I suppose I am saying, "I know I am like I am but I can enjoy you as you are, and hopefully you can enjoy me as I am."'

In 1999 Alison became pregnant and eagerly looked forward to motherhood. Later on she was to tell the author with pride that her son was 'her best creation', but there were dark moments such as the time when a woman accosted her (then obviously pregnant) and said, 'Don't you think you should get rid of it in case it turns out like you?'

However, others took the opposite view including the well-known artist and sculptor Marc Quinn.

'One day Marc, who was doing a series of sculptures of disabled people, telephoned me out of the blue to ask if I would model for him,'

Alison explains. 'I said, "You won't be interested, I'm pregnant." But he jumped at the opportunity to have a disabled and pregnant model. He took plaster casts of me so the sculpture really is me down to my toenails and hair.'

In the first week of the new millennium Alison gave birth to her son by Caesarean section at the Worthing Hospital. She named him Parys after the mythological Trojan prince who was renowned for his beauty.

'When they put Parys on my chest in the recovery room it blew my mind,' Alison recalls. 'He lay on my breast and I could touch him with my shoulder.'

When she returned to her bungalow at Shoreham in West Sussex she had a live-in nanny to help her and she was angered by suggestions that she could not look after Parys properly. When a letter appeared in the correspondence column of a newspaper suggesting that Alison was a financial liability, she wrote back: 'I and other people like me are only disabled in the eyes of society. I am financially self-sufficient and intend to remain so, bringing up my son Parys to the best of my ability...'

After Parys was born Alison agreed to appear in a documentary which, filmed through the year, appears each January in the 'A Child of Our Time' programme so that long before her statue became news she had become a 'BBC face'.

Alison's first 'royal' connection was when she went to Buckingham Palace to receive her MBE for services to art in 2003.

'When I first heard about it I thought someone was playing a joke on me,' she says. 'When I knew it was genuine the hardest thing was to keep it a secret until it was announced officially in the New Year's Honours List.

'I booked a white limo for the great day in which I travelled up to London with three friends. It was a great occasion to go the palace and be shown into the gallery where there was the royal collection of paintings to look at while I waited my turn. A royal page looked after me

– you have to stand for quite a long time before you are called out to meet the Queen so I was able to sit down while he stood in my place.

'Beforehand you are told about the protocol, the bowing and how to address the Queen. When the time came the page escorted me as it is nerve-racking to walk out in front of two hundred people. I was worried about falling over but he whispered, "Don't worry, I'll pick you up."

'I found the Queen to be incredible. She had 190 honours to give out that day to recipients ranging from me to service people, yet she remembers about you and speaks fluently about your subject. She spoke to me about art and asked about my work – and then probably had to jump to engineering or something equally different with the next recipient.

'When it was over my friends and I had lunch at the Savoy and as there were others there who had received honours it rounded off a very special day I shall remember for the rest of my life.'

Then on Christmas Day 2004 she appeared in Community Television's "The Alternative Queen's Speech", complete with a sparkling tiara, which gave her an opportunity to speculate on what beneficial projects could have been undertaken with the money spent on a war justified by a threat of weapons of mass destruction which were in fact non-existent.

Meanwhile the Greater London Council had put forward the idea that the empty plinth – the fourth plinth – in Trafalgar Square should be a platform for a piece of modern art and held a competition for such works. Marc Quinn entered the sculpture for which Alison had modelled although she believed the subject was too controversial for it to have a chance.

'I was on a beach in South Africa, where I had been advising a travel company on special safaris for the disabled, when I got a phone call from Marc to say that we had won and the statue would be set up in Trafalgar Square,' Alison says. 'From then on the phone did not stop ringing. Up until then I had regarded it as a piece of art, now I say, "I am the model that got out of her box."

'When my personal story came out in the Press neither I nor Marc were prepared for the impact. There was – and is – a lot of controversy over it. There were threats to pull it down when it was erected and The Sun's headline was "Vulgar Trafalgar" though I did get an apology. Others were delighted that a non-traditional sculpture should be set up on the fourth plinth. I saw it as a very positive platform for the disabled, a recognition that disabled people have always been part of society and always will be, and have a great deal to offer, given the chance.

'I visited Italy to see the final statue being hand carved from Marc's plaster figure. My five-year-old son is taller than me, so to see myself FOUR times larger than life shaped in the same white marble that Michelangelo used was awesome.'

Alison's young son Parys did not quite know what to think about such a big statue of his mum being erected in the heart of London but he did complain, 'Mummy, you can't see my face!' This was because he knew that when the statue was cast he was inside his mother's tummy.

For Alison, 2005 could be described as a hectic year; not only did she appear on television and see a statue of herself unveiled in London's most famous square but also her autobiography "My Life in My Hands" aroused deep interest in Britain and became a best-seller in Germany, France and Scandinavia. Such activity suggests someone full of drive and Alison is known for the energy she invests in everything she tackles. Yet while she refuses to let her disability hinder her art and associated projects, there are times when she has to give in to it.

'Some days it catches up with me and I have to stay in bed when I can't move,' she admits. 'There is an idea about people born like me that our bodies remain static over the years but unfortunately that is not so. For example, I now have to put up with arthritis and I sometimes use an electric wheelchair when I am tired which I didn't need a few years ago. On the

other hand I am lucky that most of the time disability does not hold me back and I am able to do such things as drive Parys to school, keep up with my artwork and give demonstrations of painting. I love to travel and my last big trip was to Shanghai for a wonderful meeting of MFPA artists from all parts of the world.

'For me the excitement about being an artist is that you never stop learning, and I have so many ideas and challenges ahead of me. Although I have had a lot of publicity over the statue and the book, I paint for the Association as much as ever and shall continue to do so. It is a wonderful occasion when we get together as a group for a week each year at Treloar College, it is like being part of a family. I teach life drawing there which I really enjoy. It is a great challenge because I have a room full of people with different standards, some of them new to the MFPA and just starting.

'Now, when I think of everything good that has happened to me, especially recently, I have to say the MFPA has been my springboard.'

The statue of Alison Lapper by Marc Quinn on its plinth in Trafalgar Square.

ALISON LAPPER

Kris Kirk
Windmill by the Lake

Kris Kirk
The Secret Woods

Sandy Kozikowska
Red Berries

Sandy Kozikowska
Pink Blooms

Alison Lapper   Icy River

Alison Lapper   Autumn Landscape

BRITISH ARTISTS

83

Alison Lapper
After the Dance

Alison Lapper
Portrait

Alison Lapper
Garden Gate

Alison Lapper   Midnight Mass

BRITISH ARTISTS

Peter Longstaff Winter Landscape

Peter Longstaff Winter Field

Edward Rainey
Explorer in the Snow

Peter Longstaff Church in Winter

BRITISH ARTISTS

Tom Yendell
Westminster Abbey

Tom Yendell
Sunflowers

Tom Yendell
Whitley Bay

Tom Yendell
Still Life

Tom Yendell   Peace Around the World

Peter Longstaff

'What matters is the picture.'

Imagine a midwinter landscape white with frost. Trees bend under the force of an icy wind blowing in from the North Sea. Gusts of rain sweep across the fields into the face of the lonely farmer driving a grey Ferguson tractor, a farmer who despite the wet and cold is without shoes.

In all weather, fair and foul, Peter Longstaff worked on his pig farm seven days a week for twenty years, and the reason for him often being barefoot was that he needed his feet and toes to control his tractor and other farming equipment. He had to work this way as he had been born without arms due to his mother having been prescribed the drug Thalidomide when she was carrying him. Today he is no longer a farmer. Instead of using his feet to control a "Fergie" tractor on a pig farm, Peter uses his toes to grasp a paintbrush – an amazing change of occupation.

After Peter was born in Stockton-on-Tees on 10 April 1961, his mother and father decided it would be best for him if special attention in regard to his disability should be kept to the absolute minimum. When it was suggested that he should be sent to a special school his mother, a very determined lady, refused to countenance it.

'When I was a baby I was taught to use my feet as hands,' Peter says. 'My mother and father encouraged me to pick things up with my toes. In fact when I was small I had no sense that I was disabled. I had two sisters and two brothers and I used to play with them as though I was a normal child. Starting school was no problem. Today it is sad that young children are not allowed out of sight, but then they could play in the street or go round the park and have adventures. We lived in a terraced house in Stockton and I went out and played in the street like any other kid so when I started school they were used to me. I used to play football, I did karate and I loved to go fishing. I had a great childhood.'

At infant school a special table was made to allow Peter to use his feet for writing and drawing, the latter subject being his favourite. This was abandoned as impractical when he went up in the school and the class would move to different rooms for different subjects. Peter's problem was solved by having two chairs, one to sit on and one facing him to write on.

Perhaps because of his disability, Peter thinks it was probably so, his mind was firmly focused on what he wanted to do with his future life.

'My uncle had a pig farm in Norfolk where I used to be taken on holidays,' he says. 'That must have given me the idea because when I left school at the age of sixteen I had it firmly in my head to be a pig farmer. My parents and I moved to Norfolk and fortunately I had a little money from The Thalidomide Trust, which went into buying a smallholding. I started the farm with two sows and in the end had 1800 pigs. In the beginning I had to do everything myself which at times was difficult, but at the end of the day I managed – you have to.'

By working long hours Peter built up his farm until he was able to buy another smallholding by which time he had people working for him while he did a lot of the tractor work.

On 6 April 1996 he married his wife Catherine, a former PA with the BBC in Birmingham, who had two children, Ben and Brogan. The couple bought a house close to the village of Roughton, where they live today, and settled down to family life, which was enlivened by the arrival of their son Milo. Everything was going as Peter wished and his pig breeding was continuing to flourish thanks to his hard work.

Towards the end of the last decade things became difficult for British pig farmers. This was due to huge imports of cheap bacon from abroad where the strict standards of pig raising observed in Britain are ignored.

'It was a horrendous time,' Peter recalls. 'I was selling bacon pigs for £16 each which had cost £56 to produce because the market was flooded with foreign bacon. In 1999 I could not afford to continue. I sold up in six weeks and I was absolutely redundant. At home I had nothing to do. I had worked seven days a week for twenty years and then – stop. Now my wife had to go out to work to support the family. It was a rough patch and I admit I was depressed as I had expected to do farming for life.'

Peter's answer to this depressing situation was to begin again by undertaking a new venture – he went to college in Norfolk to study art and photography. As a boy he had greatly enjoyed drawing but once he had his pig farm he had little time for such a hobby. Now his enthusiasm returned and he worked with the same energy he had put into his previous occupation. He began his new career by painting in watercolour, went on to acrylics but found his favourite medium when he decided to use oil paints.

It was Martin Johnson, head of The Thalidomide Trust, who mentioned the possibility of him joining the Association of Mouth and Foot Painting Artists and contacted Tom Yendell to make enquiries. As a result Tom, a fellow victim of Thalidomide whose story is told in this book, visited Peter to look at his work and explain the workings of the MFPA. He fired Peter with the ambition to join the Association, and to this end the ex-farmer worked tirelessly to produce samples of his painting that would be of a sufficiently high standard to submit for assessment.

'I was granted a scholarship in September 2002,' Peter says. 'Being accepted by the Association gave me an incentive to become a professional painter. I know where I am going now and what I want to be. My goal is to become a full member and I just have to try harder, and then try even harder.

'Looking back on it, the change in my career was a good thing. I really enjoy artwork and I have made a lot of new friends with MFPA people. Steven Chambers lives quite close and became a good friend. It was he who explained the workings of the Association to me in the beginning. Another good friend who has given me good advice on painting is Trevor Wells. Sometimes I scan one of my pictures and e-mail it to him for his opinion.

'In order to improve my technique I go to college as a guest, the lecturer allows me come to his lectures all day on Thursdays.'

Knowing the importance of producing paintings suitable for greeting cards Peter has specialized in producing pictures that have a Christmas theme and at the same time have an original element. One of his favourite paintings shows a town square beneath a louring winter sky with the lights of shops reflected on the snow across which shoppers hurry while carol-singers stand in a circle personifying the Yuletide atmosphere.

'I have never classed myself as disabled,' says Peter. 'I like to be sociable and I have joined a gym for a work-out a couple of times a week as I miss the exercise I had when I was farming. It is necessary to keep my legs working and luckily the family enjoys walking. We do this together at weekends when I sometimes take photographs of scenes that might be useful to me later. My aim is to be accepted in society as a professional painter. At the end of the day a picture comes from you. It doesn't matter how you do it, whether by hand, mouth or foot, what matters is the picture itself.'

Edward Rainey

'Art isn't in your hands, it's in your mind.'

Using his mouthstick with a sculpting tool attached to the end of it, Edward Rainey painstakingly smoothed a tiny line in the terracotta head that was positioned in front of his wheelchair. Then he laid the mouthstick to one side and gazed at his completed handiwork; the face of the famous Roman Catholic mystic Father Pio gazed serenely back at him. It was a moment that Eddie had dreamed about for weeks and now he was beyond words.

'I was filled with elation,' he said later. 'Father Pio had been a great inspiration to me and to sculpt his head was like an act of faith.'

This was in September 2004 and almost immediately Eddie was admitted to hospital for a surgical operation. To him the sculpture was such an important project that everything else was pushed aside including his health, the work having taken him seven weeks not counting time spent on preliminary drawings. He was to remain in the spinal unit of Glasgow's General Hospital for the next seven months, but he found some consolation in the fact that during this period a number of his paintings were being exhibited in the Mitchell Library.

As a young man it had never entered Eddie's head that one day he would be an artist. Looking back on his early life, he says, 'I had an ordinary happy childhood with my younger brother and older sister at our home in Pollok. After leaving school I worked in a butcher's until one day it struck me that there was more to life than working inside all the time. I wanted adventure and I thought the way to get it was to join the Royal Highland Fusiliers. And I certainly got it. I did abseiling. I made parachute jumps. I leapt from helicopters. I took a ski instructor's course... and I served for five-and-a-half months in Northern Ireland. That was an experience in itself.'

In 1986, on leave from the army, Eddie went to Spain with a friend to 'enjoy his last bachelor holiday.' It seemed he had everything to live for. He was twenty-four years old, he was tremendously fit, he loved army life and he was due to be married.

Remembering that sun-drenched Mediterranean day he says, 'After arriving at our hotel in Marbella and unpacking our bags, my friend Edward and I – we were known as "the two Eddies" – could not wait to have a swim. We raced down to the pool. I was in such a hurry that I dived into the shallow end by mistake and struck my head on the bottom. I remember the noise of the impact was like a muffled grenade and in that second I lost all control of my body. Luckily I had enough presence of mind to hold my breath until someone realized what had happened and got me out.'

Eddie was so seriously injured that he was flown to Glasgow by air ambulance and taken to the Western Infirmary. There his distraught mother and father were advised that their son could not last more than three days, as the effect of the accident had been to sever his spinal cord. A priest hurried to his bedside and gave him the last rites.

The three days went by and he was still alive, and as more days passed his doctors were amazed at the hold he kept on life. Then his parents were told that although he had survived, movement would never return to his limbs. And this time the diagnosis was correct.

'What saved me was that I was as fit as a fiddle and I have the army to thank for that,' Eddie explains. 'Service life gives you an attitude that sustains you regardless of what happens. But having been so physically active I found the immobilization hard to cope with once it became clear that, although I was paralysed, I was going to survive. I was so depressed that I cried an ocean at the beginning. I kept asking "Why me?" but later I answered myself with "Why not me?"'

If it was Eddie's military background that supported him in the touch-and-go days after his accident, he believes that it was his spiritual reawakening that gave him the strength to cope with the dreary times that followed.

'I remember in hospital being put in a wheelchair and left alone for hours and hours in front of a window looking down on a car-park, when what I desperately wanted was someone to talk to,' he says.

Sometimes a book was put in front of him but it was of little use as he was unable to turn the pages.

'Thinking back to that time I don't know how I came through it,' he muses. 'What I do know is that I did not do it by myself. It was as though there was somebody pulling me through the shadows. God helps you through your life every day even if you don't want to believe it. It was about nine years ago that I realized this and began to experience an overwhelming sensation of joy and love. I didn't know what it was but it kept getting stronger.

'At first I was afraid to tell my family because I didn't know what it was myself. I told them when I eventually understood that it was the presence of God that inspired these feelings. Although baptized a Roman Catholic, I had become non-practising but since then I go to Mass and find the spiritual comfort that comes with the Communion. This helps me to keep on at what I am doing.'

At last came the great day when, after months of specialized treatment, Eddie was allowed to return to his parents' home. Yet after the joy of the reunion he found that life in a wheelchair was far from happy. The flat in which they lived was on the fourth floor of a tenement that made it so difficult for him to be taken downstairs – there was no lift – he hardly ever went out.

'I felt I had to do something other than stare out of the window or watch television,' he says. 'I desperately needed something positive in my life and then, just at the right time, my aunt gave me a calendar from the Association of Mouth and Foot Painting Artists. Looking at it I felt encouraged to try painting myself and so I began mouth painting by making charcoal sketches. When I was able to control a brush I went on to oil paints. I also tried putting on the colours with a palette knife but this turned out to be too difficult.

'What really encouraged me in the early days was when my mother proudly showed one of my pictures to a neighbour who turned to her and said, "Are you sure you didn't do that, Cathy?" It was then that I wanted painting to become more than a pastime and once I started seriously I found there was not enough time in the day. After four years I believed that I had reached a good enough standard to submit my work to the MFPA and as a result I was granted a scholarship.

'My next goal is to become a full member, not just from the financial aspect but also as an honour not only to myself but those around me. An accident like mine affects everybody. Your family suffers as much as you do so it is a wonderful thing when they can share something good with you. You have to have such targets to strive for.'

In his quest for improving his painting skills Eddie attends art classes at the Langside College, and it was here that the idea of sculpting as well as painting was born.

His first attempt with the terracotta was a study of a pair of flames appearing to rise from the ground. This gave him the feel of the various small sculpting tools that could be attached to the end of his mouthstick. After this he made a number of sketches from photographs of Father Pio at different angles and these became the blueprints for the work.

'I started with a large block of terracotta clay in front of me and imagined the head inside it,' he explains. 'Then, working four hours a day,

EDWARD RAINEY

I gradually scraped away the excess clay until finally the complete head emerged and was then fired in a kiln for three days. To me it proved my belief that art isn't in your hands, it's in your mind.'

While in hospital after his operation Eddie planned that apart from continuing his painting when he was released, he would tackle a "lifetime" project, an undertaking no less than the sculptured figures for the Stations of the Cross. It is a work that he estimates will take him at least two years and which he hopes will find a place in Glasgow's Roman Catholic cathedral.

Today Eddie lives at ground level in a house close to his parents, which enables him to be looked after by his mother Cathy. She is a small slim lady with an abundance of humour and a heart-warming love for her son who refers to her as 'my wee ma'.

'At times I enjoy a wonderful sense of peace and I am happier than I was before the accident,' he declares. 'It has made me a better person spiritually. Life is one big mystery but I feel that there is something within me that no earthly thing can touch. I also believe that goodness never dies in people but moves on.'

Robert Trent

'We all need to have targets.'

'Can you move it a bit to the left, I want to get that fallen log in the picture,' said Robert Trent, watching the tiny screen of the digital camera.

Kim Trent moved the camera a slight fraction and her husband said, 'That's great. Take it, please.'

It was a typical weekend activity for the Trent family, a countryside outing combined with a quest for scenes for Rob's paintbrush.

'That old farmhouse over there might make a good picture,' said his daughter Yasmin. 'Let's take a look.'

They turned and set off along a bridle path accompanied by their excited Yorkshire terrier, Rob leading the way in his wheelchair. The reason for the wheelchair is that Rob was born without functioning muscles in his arms and legs. Like some other artists mentioned in this book, he was a victim of the rare condition known as arthrogryposis.

'I was born in 1959 and I stayed at home for the first six years,' he explains. 'To begin with I was able to walk with callipers but later I found it much safer in a wheelchair as I had a tendency to fall over. I had three brothers and as all of us had been born within a period of five years we were very close.

'When I was five I had a tutor who came to our house and she helped me to learn to write with a pencil held in my mouth. She was very impressed by the Association of Mouth and Foot Painting Artists so I knew about it early on.

'At six I was sent to the Chailey Heritage home for the disabled where Alison Lapper grew up. At first I found it very traumatic as I missed my family that was now 150 miles away. At six you don't really know what's happening but in the end you get used to it.

'At Chailey the focus was not so much on the academic side as learning to cope with disability and preparation for the outside world. In some ways it was hard going but it toughened me up and now I appreciate it. After Chailey I moved to Hereward College in Coventry where I got my A-Levels, though not in art. Finally I enrolled at the Southampton Institution of Higher Education where I obtained my BSc in information systems.'

The fact that Rob used his mouth to hold a pencil and later a mouthstick to work computer keys did not hold him back as far as work was concerned. He soon obtained a job at the Southampton headquarters of the Ordnance Survey where today he is Web Operations Manager. Two years after he started work he decided to continue his studies and took evening classes. At school he had been keen on painting but with work and study this had to be reluctantly laid aside.

One of Rob's abiding interests is football and not long after he had completed his university course he and a group of fellow fans took a coach trip north to see their team play. After the match they continued on to Blackpool to spend the rest of the weekend there. On the coach Rob found himself sitting next to an attractive girl named Kim. They enjoyed talking together and as the weekend progressed a friendship began to develop between them. When the fans returned home Rob asked her if he could take her out on a date. She agreed, and two years later they were married. In May 2005 they celebrated their tenth wedding anniversary.

Their daughter Yasmin was born in September 1994. Today her favourite subject is art and often father and daughter enjoy painting sessions together.

'Life had been pretty full but the old itch to paint returned and I began again,' Rob explains. 'Then, about eight years ago, I sent off some of my work to the MFPA and before long I was accepted as a student.'

With the encouragement this gave him he attended a series of Saturday art classes and when the course ended his teacher advised him to continue with a private tutor and suggested an artist named Ron Milson. By coincidence, he lived only four doors away from Rob and so home tuition began, an arrangement that has worked very well over the years.

'Ron has been a great tutor who has given me a lot of encouragement but who is not afraid to criticize,' says Rob. 'I began painting with watercolours but I have moved on to oils which are more forgiving and allow me to go back to a picture once I have thought it over. I particularly like winter landscapes, which are suitable for Christmas cards. I was delighted when one of my pictures was chosen by the MFPA to be in their 2003 calendar. The following year my picture of the Houses of Parliament with Big Ben at night was chosen to be a Christmas card.'

Working office hours Rob cannot spend as much time at his easel as he would like but he still reckons the hours he manages to fit in is equal to a couple of days a week.

'I am happy with the progress I have been making allowing for the amount of time I have available,' he says. 'Ultimately I want to paint full-time but my immediate target is to become an associate member. I think we all need to have targets to aim for in life.'

One of Rob's targets was to learn to drive. Today the car provides freedom of movement for the able-bodied undreamt of by past generations and it not only gives mobility to the wheelchair-bound but also a sense of independence. It is no wonder it had long been Rob's target to get his own form of transport. In 2004 a van was adapted to his special requirements and in less than a year of learning and practising he passed his driving test.

'I can't measure what it has meant to me,' he declares. 'To be able to drive to work is great but better still I can repay the favours I received from people who gave me transport by sharing journeys. And now that I can drive, Kim and I go on trips looking for suitable landscape scenes to paint which she takes on the digital camera and I process through my computer. Sometimes I take several scenes and take a bit of each and paint a composite picture.'

Digital cameras are a boon to disabled artists who want to paint outdoor scenes. Most would like to set up their easels and paint on the spot but this presents difficulties for those without the use of their limbs who cannot even brush away annoying flies or stinging insects.

'I thoroughly enjoy painting and it is my greatest wish to become a full-time painter,' Rob says and adds in a philosophical mood, 'I cannot say that my disability has held me back, in fact it has made me more determined than I might have been if I were able-bodied.'

Trevor Wells

'I like to do scenes that you could walk into.'

'As far as art was concerned the art period at school was a lesson in which you did as little as possible,' says Trevor Wells, one of the best-known English mouth painting artists. 'All I was really interested in was sport. I was mad about it. Strangely enough, I still am though now I can only watch.'

On leaving school in the summer of 1973 Trevor, who had been born in Portsmouth in 1956, became an apprentice carpenter, completing his apprenticeship in 1976. Then the highlight of his week was to play for the Uxbridge Rugby Club. The exhilaration of the game and the camaraderie that is traditionally associated with rugger players became one of the chief factors, if not the chief factor, in the young man's life.

In September 1978 Trevor's team set out for the grounds of the Twickenham Rugby Club where a 'beer match' – a Sunday game, for the uninitiated – had been arranged. Perhaps because it was a fun event Trevor did not take it as seriously as he should have done.

'It was a terribly hot Indian summer,' he remembers. 'We were not keyed up before the game as usually happens. Normally you never put your boots on when you are on the pitch but this time we did, which shows our relaxed mood.

'The opposition kicked off and put the ball straight into touch so we chose to have a scrum on the halfway line. I was playing hooker in the front row and must have been late putting my head down into the scrum and hit the top of my head on the incoming scrum. When the scrum broke up I collapsed to the floor unable to move.'

Trevor was rushed by ambulance to London's Middlesex Hospital where it was found that his neck was broken at the C4 level. That evening he was transferred to Charing Cross Hospital for a spinal infusion and later taken to Stoke Mandeville Hospital, world famous for its treatment of spinal injuries. He remained there for seven months where he strove to come to the terms with the fact that in those few seconds on the Rugby pitch his life had completely changed.

'I like to think that I did not find it too difficult to accept that I was now totally disabled,' he says. 'Of course it is hard to say so yourself, but I realized that I must not have the attitude of some who felt the whole world was against them because of an accident.

'Having to cope with a quadriplegic would have been too big a burden for my mother so in April 1979 I was transferred to the Alderbourne Unit at a hospital on the outskirts of London. It had only recently been opened and was designed to cater for long-term patients like me.'

Like Grant Sharman who suffered a similar accident in New Zealand, Trevor's enthusiasm for Rugby remained undimmed and he watched it avidly on television and read the sports section in the newspapers, turning the pages with a mouthstick. In this way the days passed without Trevor doing anything except to follow his favourite sport. At times he was troubled by the thought that he was leading an empty existence but, he asked himself, what could he do to alter his life? There seemed to be no answer.

'Then someone suggested that I should have a go at painting,' he says. 'It was something I had never considered. I had no interest in art and painting was the last thing at which I thought I would be any good. On the other hand it would help to pass the time and I agreed to try. A paintbrush was fitted to my mouthstick, paints were laid out in front of me and I began. I must admit the result was pretty iffy but when I was on my third picture I was amazed – I was actually painting!'

One reason he found little difficulty in using a paintbrush was because he had his mouthstick attached to a Rugby gum shield to distribute the weight evenly in his mouth. Thus no undue stress was placed upon the teeth as can happen when they are clamped on a pencil or brush handle for long periods. As for the mouthstick itself, Trevor had an extremely light arrow shaft fitted to the gum shield and this device proved so effective that his writing is far neater today than when he was able to do it by hand.

It is typical of Trevor that when he talks about his painting methods he makes it sound as though there is nothing to it.

'There are so few rules,' he says with cheerful confidence. 'You just have to remember that you start with the background and work forward, that light against dark throws up colour and so on.'

It sounds almost effortless but the reality was that Trevor had to strive very hard to learn his craft, teaching himself by seemingly endless trial and error. The possibility of becoming a professional artist never occurred to him, it was his love of painting that continually urged him to improve his technique.

By chance relatives of a fellow patient in the unit became interested in Trevor's work and, having seen greeting cards published by the Mouth and Foot Painting Artists, suggested that he should get in touch with the Association. Although he had never heard of the organization, Trevor followed their advice. As a result he became a student in 1984 and two-and-a-half years later he was made a full member.

'I certainly could not survive on my own but through its marketing the Association makes it possible for me to earn a living with my paintbrush,' Trevor explains. 'And I am lucky in that the scenes I like painting are commercial. It takes me a long time to complete a picture so I can see no point in working for weeks on end on a painting if it is not suitable for printing.'

'I do like snow scenes. With the light snow reflects you can get some lovely effects. Winter transforms everything and to me there is something magical about snowdrifts with the footmarks of animals printed on them, even the tyremarks on a snow covered road.'

It can take up to four months for Trevor to complete a painting which seems a long time even for a mouth painter but his pictures are built up with almost microscopic detail. He jokes that in order to get this effect some of his brushes have only two hairs.

Looking at his landscapes one gets the impression that every leaf on every tree is individually painted. This gives the effect of great clarity and reflects Trevor's dictum: 'I like to do scenes that you could walk into.'

In July 1990 Trevor left the Alderbourne Unit to marry his wife Shirley whom he had met when she became his osteopath.

In recounting how she met Trevor, Shirley Wells once said, 'I am an osteopath and was once asked if I could treat someone in a wheelchair. I replied that it would be no problem and soon afterwards Trevor arrived. We rapidly became friends and very, very soon I no longer saw him in a wheelchair.

'A lot of people might think it mundane doing the little things that I have to do for him but it is the involvement that I like. We chat about things, discuss how a picture is going, what should be here and what should be there. This is much nicer than if you are married to a solicitor or someone like that where you cannot get involved with their work. When Trevor goes to exhibitions I obviously go with him and again I am involved. The public are quite surprised to find that we are just a normal couple – then they lose the wheelchair and see us as we really are.'

Although his accident obviously put an end to Trevor's involvement in physical sports, the old sporting thrill returned when he arranged to have his first flight in a glider – much to Shirley's misgiving.

'She's never been openly keen about flying in general but she thought it was a bit mad to go up in an aircraft with no engine,' Trevor explains. 'But I found it a wonderful experience to fly over beautiful terrain without any noise apart from the slight hiss of the air over the wings.'

The year 2000 was celebrated as the Millennium Year but to Trevor it had much deeper significance. With Shirley he travelled to Sydney in order to represent Britain at a convention of MFPA delegates from around the world.

'As part of the proceedings, and to my great delight, I was unanimously nominated by the board to join their ranks, a motion supported by all the delegates,' Trevor recalls. 'This vote of confidence in me was a great honour and a moment I shall treasure forever.'

In this role Trevor has to visit the Association's international headquarters in Liechtenstein in December and June each year for board meetings at which Association matters are discussed and decisions taken democratically. Looking back on his life as a professional artist and his involvement in the MFPA, Trevor says reflectively, 'No way would I have become a painter if my accident had not happened and to progress to being one of the artists' representatives on the board of an international company is just fantastic. It has also allowed me to travel around the world to places such as Copenhagen, Prague, Vienna, Atlanta, Vancouver, Taiwan and Sydney.'

Recently Trevor and his wife Shirley bought a lovely 200-year-old farmhouse in Menorca from which they can commute easily to England for meetings and exhibitions, as it is only a short flight away. Trevor says that apart from the convenience of it being a ground floor only house and its pleasant surrounding, there is another advantage. He explains, 'Where we lived in England we were too far away from the pub and other facilities to go by foot and wheelchair. Here we are in easy distance of the nearby tapas bar to go for a leisurely drink without having to drive.'

TREVOR WELLS

Tom Yendell

'A focal point.'

In the 18th century Gilbert White, a local clergyman wrote "The Natural History and Antiquities of Selborne", which has never been out of print since it was published in 1789. Today his house, known as "The Wakes", is The Gilbert White Museum, which draws great numbers of visitors to this typically English Hampshire village. Another attraction is the MFPA Art Gallery in which members' paintings and prints are displayed and special exhibitions are frequently held. Listed among the established attractions of the area in the local guidebook, the gallery is presided over by Tom Yendell who also paints without the use of his hands.

Tom's story goes back over four decades to when Thalidomide was causing numerous handicapped babies to be born. As a result of the infamous drug Tom came into the world in 1962 without arms.

'When I was born I was quickly taken away from my mother,' Tom recalls. '"Where are you taking my baby?" she demanded. "You won't get him back," said a nurse. My poor mother thought that she meant ever. The reason that I was whisked away was because I had a collapsed lung but I think there was also anxiety about a mother's reaction to having a baby boy with no arms.

'As it turned out my mother and father took my disability remarkably well. They did not treat me differently from other members of the family.

'When I was eight a Dr Wilkie, who was also without arms, came over from America. He visited us and showed me how he did normal everyday things. He was very successful, drove a car and had a family. This gave my parents a boost as they saw that, like him, it was possible their son could lead a normal life.'

It seemed quite natural to Tom to use his feet as other children used their hands. Later as an artist he painted not only by gripping a brush with his toes but also by holding it between his teeth. Both methods are equally effective.

Tom's father, an ex-Royal Marine, had a bakery in Leighton Buzzard and was famous for his cake decoration and wedding cakes. At the time arthritis forced him to give up this work the Lady Hoare Trust, which was concerned with Thalidomide children, was looking for a couple to run its special holiday home at Pevensey in East Sussex. Tom's parents took the post and Tom attended a local primary school. Here his progress was not satisfactory so at the age of nine he went to a prep school after which he was enrolled at Lord Mayor Treloar College in Hampshire, which was to have a great influence on his life.

The college dates back to 1908 when Lord Mayor Treloar of the City of London saw the need for children with respiratory complaints to go to a home in the country where they could benefit from clean air. It began as a hospital at Alton and later expanded with the purchase of an estate on which the college was established.

When Tom went to Treloar there were eighty students, today it is the biggest school for the disabled in Britain with around three hundred young students, most of whom are boarders, who study for their GCSEs and A-Levels.

After he had been there seven years Tom decided that his best subject was art and he undertook a foundation year at the Hastings College of Art, going on to an Expressive Art course at Brighton Polytechnic. It was at this time that he obtained his first car, a specially adapted Mini, in which he passed his driving test and gained a new sense of freedom.

An important development, one which was to have a profound effect on Tom's future life, came when he decided to take a sabbatical year after two years of studying art.

He was finding it hard to concentrate and with this came the realization that he needed a change of activity. To this end he went to work for the charity known as CRYPT, which stands for "Creative Young People Together". The aim of CRYPT is to help young handicapped people who show artistic ability, providing them with accommodation in bungalows around the country. Since then a feature of Tom's life has been to provide help and encouragement for fellow handicapped persons.

When half of his sabbatical year had passed in this way Tom returned to Treloar College to assist his old teacher in the art room. Sadly for Tom his mentor died so he carried on giving lessons single-handed. During this period he became interested in photography but found obvious difficulties in using a camera. The only way he could focus was by bending down and holding the camera with his feet while he peered through the viewfinder. The solution to the problem was to design a shoulder device to which the camera is attached, enabling him to operate it comfortably by means of his chin and mouth.

At the end of his sabbatical Tom returned to the Polytechnic where he gained his degree.

With college days over Tom went to work for an organization connected with small, newly formed companies named "Business in the Community". This meant commuting each day to London from his home in Lewes but, although he enjoyed the work, the daily travel became too much for him and he had to resign.

Several years earlier, when he had been doing his foundation course, Tom had got in touch with the MFPA and in reply had been asked to contact them again when his studies were completed. This seemed to be a good time to do so and, after his work had been assessed, the Association granted him a scholarship in March 1986, becoming a full member ten years later.

The next big event in Tom's life was to buy an old house on the Sussex Downs romantically named "Hunter's Moon". It badly needed renovation but that did not deter Tom who had a very good reason for moving in.

'It had a great studio at the bottom of the garden and I really enjoyed doing it up,' he explains. 'I was planning to get married to Lucy who I had met the year before when she was doing her foundation course in art. The house was to be ready for her when she finished her art degree in graphics and illustration at Bath.'

Although this was a busy time for Tom he still managed to do voluntary work for maladjusted children at the local school. It was for such work that he was chosen as one of the "Men of the Year" and received his citation in London with such celebrities as Richard Branson, Bob Monkhouse and Frank Bruno.

Sometimes people have said to Tom's mother, 'You must be proud of your son.'

'She never admits it,' said Tom. 'I suppose she is so used to me that she merely replies, "Just what I expected of him." On one occasion I was interviewed on the Midweek radio programme. It was a last-minute arrangement and Mum knew nothing about it. She was in the kitchen washing coffee cups when she turned on the radio and heard someone talking about his life and how he managed without arms. Mum was greatly interested because he was a Thalidomide case just like her son and she said later that listening to him made her feel really good. At the end of the programme there was the usual credits and when it came to "Thanks to Tom Yendell" she was so amazed she nearly fell over.'

Tom and Lucy were married on the eighth day of August 1988, Tom joking that he had chosen the date of 8.8.88, as it would help him to remember his wedding anniversary. Lucy opted for a honeymoon in Iceland despite Tom's doubts.

'I was rather apprehensive about going,' he says, 'but it turned out to be a wonderful experience.

We spent seven days touring the country and the rest of the time in Reykjavik. I was so impressed by the Icelanders' attitude to the disabled. They have a Union of Disabled People which owns a specially designed building where the disabled can rent apartments.'

The following year Tom returned to Treloar College to take up the new position of part-time activities co-ordinator, a job that suited him as it allowed him to continue with his art in which he began to specialize in painting on silk. This meant that the couple reluctantly left 'Hunter's Moon' and settled in Holybourne which was close to the college. Here their two children, Joe and Holly, were born.

For some time Tom had been thinking that a permanent art gallery to exhibit the work of MFPA members would not only be of interest to the public but also act as an artistic centre for the painters themselves. One day when he was driving through Selborne he saw a 'For sale' sign on a building at the part of the village known as The Plestor. In his fertile mind's eye Tom saw how it could be transformed into an attractive gallery. With typical enthusiasm he put up the idea to the Association with the result that the property was acquired and he was given the go-ahead to develop it. In 1992 Tom's dream became a reality when the gallery was opened and since then he has been its curator.

'We used to get the benefit of visitors coming to see Gilbert White's village,' he says. 'Now people come specially to see the gallery.'

Visitors cannot fail to be impressed when they view the array of the pictures on display; pictures that give no hint as to how they have been painted. As Erich Stegmann once said, 'What difference does it make how a picture is painted? A painter does not only mean a pair of hands – he paints from his heart what his eyes see.'

Apart from displaying original paintings, the gallery has a wide range of prints for sale including examples of the work of MFPA artists from different parts of the world. It also has other functions as Tom explains, 'The gallery acts as a base from which we organize talks on the work of the Association. Schools and bodies that would like to have a speaker from the MFPA contact us here.

'Another aspect of the gallery is that it gives the artists a focal point. Isolation was a problem that used to affect foot and mouth painters, especially those severely disabled who rarely left their homes. They worked in a vacuum. They would paint, send off their work to the Association, and start the next picture. What they lacked was contact with fellow artists with whom they could talk about their work.

'One of the great advantages of Selborne is that it is close to Treloar College where the artists now get together once a year when the regular students are on holiday. They have painting workshops and come to the gallery where special exhibitions are arranged. This gives them a chance to see the work of fellow members in these surroundings.'

In July 2002 the Selborne gallery received royal recognition when Tom arranged a visit by HRH The Prince of Wales accompanied by the Lord Lieutenant of Hampshire. Rob Trent demonstrated the technique of mouth painting and Prince Charles who, as an enthusiastic artist himself, showed great interest in the technique and discussed painting with several MFPA artists who were present. Under the pseudonym of "Arthur George Carrick", the Prince has exhibited at the Royal Academy, the name being part of his official title, which includes Earl of Carrick.

The year 2002 was one of great significance to Tom. It was the year of his fortieth birthday and, despite medical predictions, he found that he is still very much alive.

'Thalidomide babies were not meant to live to forty,' he explains. 'The drug manufacturer's medical experts said we were not going to reach that age so they could keep the compensation down. Around fifteen hundred Thalidomide babies were born, a thousand of which did not survive and their parents received no compensation. The curious thing is that those of us who did survive appear to have a slightly higher life expectancy than normal.'

Apart from his own silk paintings and work in the gallery, Tom does a great deal of public relations work on behalf of the MFPA and the disabled in general through lectures, radio talks and television appearances. Readers will have noticed that in some other chapters Tom's name has been mentioned by artists telling of his help and guidance in joining the MFPA. Thanks to reality television "Big Brother" has a dubious connotation, yet in the nicest possible way it describes Tom who has been a 'big brother' to new recruits to the Association.

Tom Yendell presenting his painting of Westminster Abbey to HRH The Duke of Edinburgh at the Mobility Roadshow.

The MFPA gallery in Selborne was honoured by a visit from HRH The Prince of Wales.

Robert Trent demonstrates his technique as HRH The Prince of Wales and Tom Yendell look on.

HRH The Prince of Wales chats with Trevor Wells, who presented him with an original painting.

HRH The Prince of Wales meets Keith Jansz and his wife Cindy.

Artists Worldwide

In more than seventy countries members of the MFPA partnership have found fulfilment through their art. Here are the stories of just a few such artists.

Iwao Adachi

'I could get over my grief when I was drawing pictures.'

To become disabled often has a devastating effect on the sufferer but when there is rejection instead of sympathy life can become unbearable. No one can understand that better that Iwao Adachi. His experience of humiliation began when he was in the fourth grade of his school in Osaka. A teacher had told his class that if one fed wild birds from when they were chicks they would remain tame as they grew. That day when he and his friends were walking home they spied a number of sparrows' nests high on the pylon of an electrical substation. One of the boys suggested that if they could get some chicks from the nests they could rear them as pets. It seemed a great idea except that the nests were too high to reach safely but jokingly they dared Iwao to try. Though inwardly reluctant, a dare was something he could not refuse.

His friends watched as he climbed higher and higher up the pylon. When he finally got close to a nest he shouted down triumphantly, 'There are sparrow chicks here...'

There was a blinding shower of sparks from the 33,000-volt cable and Iwao plunged to earth head first. As he lay crumpled on the ground the horrified boys believed he was dead.

When he finally recovered consciousness the first thing he became aware of were the distressed faces of his mother and father staring down at him. Behind them crowded hospital doctors, policemen and journalists.

'Doctors said it was a miracle that I survived,' Iwao says today. 'The electric current ran through my body from my right hand and created a hole in my abdomen the size of my fist while my head was injured as a result of the fall. And all my body was burned black. My right hand was amputated and after two operations I lost my right arm from the shoulder and my left from the elbow.'

Iwao Adachi had been born in 1939 in Osaka where he lived happily with his family until their house was burnt down in an American air raid. The family then moved to the home of his aunt from where he went to school, which he thoroughly enjoyed until his accident. As a result of his injuries he was to remain in hospital for four months but on being discharged his homecoming was not the joyous occasion he might have expected.

'It was miserable because it was as though I was a piece of wood,' he says. 'My mother burst into tears and my father looked away from me and kept silent. I was unable to go to school; I could not dress or feed myself. I could not live for a single day without my mother's help.'

A year later a second tragedy struck the eleven-year-old boy. His mother, on whom he was so dependent, died of a heart attack. She had suffered from a heart condition and it was believed that her son's dreadful accident had aggravated it. Shortly afterwards his father's work called him away and the boy was left alone in his aunt's house.

'She was a hard person and did not help me as my mother had,' he says. 'I remember one day how I struggled to put on my trousers by myself. I was lying on the floor, trying to work my way into them, when my friends dropped in to see me on their way to school. "What are you doing like that?" they demanded.

'It was obvious but I was ashamed. They left and I restarted work on my trousers. After two hours I had worked them up on to my hips but I could not manage the hook, as my mouth could not reach it. Tears of vexation filled my eyes.

My aunt was in the next room but she did not help me. Then by pressing against the corner of a desk and using what remained of my left arm, I managed to fix the hook. My joy at this achievement was but a passing moment. There came the need to go to the toilet and I found that to undo the hook was as hard as it had been to fix it. At the last moment I rushed into the water closet. There the thought of having to struggle to get my trousers up again made me want to cry. I just wanted to sit there forever...

'After a while one of my friends visited me on the way back from school and found me standing in my underpants. "What's the matter with you?" he asked. "You are still as you were. What have you done the whole day?"

'"I tried to put on my trousers..." Then I could find no more words.'

The shame that Iwao felt at not being able to look after himself had the effect of making him strive to be independent. He taught himself to do many of the everyday things of life, even needlework and drawing by using his mouth to hold a needle or a pencil. This self-sufficiency was inspired by his father once telling him the story of Junkyo Ohishi, a true story that he has never forgotten.

One of the most remarkable mouth painters of her day, Junkyo Ohishi died in 1968 at the age of eighty having spent many years of her life as a third-rank Buddhist priestess in the temple district of Bukoin in Kyoto. She had lost her hands when she was seventeen when, in a fit of insanity, her stepfather attacked those about him with a sword. Later she said, 'One day I saw a small bird feeding its youngster with its beak. That was what prompted me to learn to draw with my mouth.'

A member of the Association of Mouth and Foot Painting Artists, Junkyo became famous in Japan for her Buddhist compassion when she opened a home offering sheltered accommodation for handicapped children.

Following the example of Junkyo, Iwao turned to drawing whenever he felt distressed.

'In the year that my mother passed away I began to draw pictures,' he says. 'It was to release my sorrow and to practise the use of mouth. At first I tried to draw straight lines, triangles or squares – it took me a year to be able to draw straight lines. After that I started to draw rough sketches and then I began using watercolours.

'I could get over my grief while I was drawing pictures, I could forget my life without arms.' Nevertheless he suffered from deep depression when not working on the scraps of paper he saved.

'I hated to be called Daruma – man without hands – and have stones thrown at me, so I exercised secretly at night.' he says. 'This later bore fruit when in the Paraplegic Games held at Yoyogi, Tokyo, I won the gold medal in the 50 metre breaststroke and a bronze medal in the standing broad jump. People said it was great – maybe, but the work that had led up to it was for surviving.'

After this Iwao moved to his father's one-room apartment, which was vacant most of the time, and with it came the necessity of earning money to support himself. To this end he tried a variety of jobs, from baby-sitting to cleaning a cinema.

'People were unwilling to employ me because I did not have arms and often I worked without payment to prove that I was capable of doing a job,' he says. 'I was thankful if someone gave me work but once I was hired I was always anxious in case I was fired. I often was and ran back home with abuse shouted after me. At one stage, when I was seventeen years old, it seemed that everything was too hard to bear and I decided I could not go on. I stood on a railway track and waited while the train came towards me with a deafening roar. At the last moment some instinct made me leap to one side.'

Two years later Iwao found regular work with the Izumiya Industries Company, which manufactured road-making equipment. Having taught himself to ride a bicycle "no hands" he was employed as a messenger at a fraction of what an able-bodied worker would earn but he was delighted to be in work.

116

It was now his ambition to try painting in oils and on 24 April 1962 – a date that is etched in his memory – he was able to buy a set of oil colours with the money that he had saved at the rate of five yen a day. As there was not enough money for him to buy a palette as well, he solved the problem by using the glass that he removed from his window after putting on all his clothing against the freezing cold of the winter nights.

In November of the same year Iwao entered an oil painting for display in a Fuse City exhibition. It was not only accepted but also sold for the seemingly astronomical sum of 6,000 yen. Recalling that wonderful day, Iwao says, 'The success overpaid me for all my efforts. I felt I could have thrown both my non-existent arms up to the sky; instead I turned a couple of somersaults. I spent 1000 yen on colours and canvases, and donated the rest to institutions for the handicapped. People said I was so poor I should have kept the money for myself but it just seemed too much for me.'

Iwao's gesture proved the parable of bread cast upon the waters. A newspaper reported how a mouth painting artist had given away most of the money he had earned from his first sale. The story was picked up by the Association of Mouth and Foot Painting Artists who have discovered many of their members through the Press. Iwao was enrolled as a student and paid a monthly stipend, which came just at the right moment as the company he worked for went bankrupt.

Two years later, in 1965, he was made a full member of the Association and his financial future was assured. Now he was able to paint as he has always wished to paint and he went from success to success with frequent exhibitions.

'There is a saying "The world is as kind as it is cruel",' says Iwao and then proceeds to tell the story of the unusual way he met his wife in 1969. In the autumn of that year he returned home from sketching Lake Biwa for a picture he wanted to enter in an exhibition. A newspaper reported how after the picture won a prize Iwao had presented it to an institution for the handicapped known as the Blue Sky Special

School with the result he was inundated with letters from readers.

'It was hard work writing answers to all of them,' he explains. 'For some unknown reason I left one unanswered. It was from a woman named Shoko Hidaka who worked in a beauty parlour. I felt very sorry that I had left her out so I found her telephone number and dialled her. "Is that Miss Hidaka?" I asked and she replied, "Ah, you are Mr Adachi." I was surprised that she knew it was me when I phoned her for the first time but from then on we had telephone conversations and exchanged letters.

'One day she phoned me and said "Please take me somewhere this Monday."

'"How about Nara Park?" I suggested. As we had never met we described ourselves and arranged to meet on the platform of Truruhashi Station. Next Monday I learned her life story in the park and we had a long conversation until we came to the temple of the great statue of Buddha where we both offered prayers. The next evening Shoko rang me up and from the other end of the line came words "If you think it would be good for you, please make me your bride. I have just phoned my mother in Kyushu and she agrees. So please marry me."

'Later I learned what she had asked of the Buddha – "I should like to live with a disabled person so please make it come true. I know hardships might lie ahead for me but that's OK."

'The great Buddha statue responded beautifully. Maybe I was not disabled in my heart and Shoko became my wife.'

In January 1970 the couple were married and towards the end of the year Shoko gave birth to a baby girl they named Emiko, the daughter whom Iwao declared 'gives me the energy for tomorrow.'

Now one of the best known artists in Japan, Iwao has come a very long way from the days when he was ridiculed for his affliction or when desperation nearly ended his life on a railway track... the world is as kind as it is cruel.

Eros Bonamini

'I have dedicated myself entirely to painting.'

The work of Eros Bonamini has won the acclaim of art critics around the world yet hardly ever is mention made of the fact that it is the work of a mouth painter. For example, a book entitled "Cronotopografie" has been published in which art experts gave their views on Bonamini's work, analysing it from every angle, yet no hint was given to the reader that Bonamini is disabled. This would have been applauded by Erich Stegmann, the founder of the MFPA, whose credo was that what appeared on the canvas was what mattered, not the method by which it got there.

Born in Verona in 1942, Eros Bonamini still has such affection for the town, that he signs his paintings with the pseudonym "Veronese". At school he studied technical subjects and had a love of mathematics, and it is doubtful if it ever crossed his mind that one day he might ever become interested in painting. Swimming and diving were his favourite sports. Then, one day in 1960, he had an accident when making a racing dive with the result that he was paralysed from the neck down. After a period in hospital he was allowed to return home where time passed slowly for the once active boy. Books and classical music became his escape from immobility.

'After the accident I often found myself alone and with a great deal of time to think,' he says. 'To pass the time I threw myself into literature and then by chance I discovered painting which opened up an entirely new vista for me. Since then I have dedicated myself entirely to painting.'

From the moment he first had the handle of a paintbrush positioned between his teeth, Eros developed his latent talent at a remarkable rate. In due course the director of a publishing house in Verona became interested when he heard of the young man who was painting by means of his mouth. He visited Eros in his home and was so impressed by the work he saw that he sent it to the Association of Mouth and Foot Painting Artists. March 1966 was a milestone in the young artist's life when he became a full member of the Association.

Although Eros began as a pictorial painter, his lively mind began considering the more abstract elements of art, especially Cubism. This artistic movement owed its origins to Picasso and Braque in 1907 and it rapidly influenced Western painting. In Cubism the artist divided the subject of his picture into a number of parts and depicted differing aspects of it on the same canvas.

Eros explains, 'Cubism has interested me because it is an operation on Time made up of the simultaneity of the artist's point of view so that an object and a landscape presented simultaneously on the same canvas shows a complex reality. And this was perhaps the start of my particular work on Time – I should say, my curiosity on the operation of Time.'

Perhaps it was his early study of mathematics that inspired him to explore the nature of Time through the medium of art. But such an exploration could not be undertaken with conventional paint and canvas, and Eros devised his own materials to undertake the quest. An idea of how he developed his materials and technique was given in an article by the well-known Italian critic Alberto Veca in which he explained that cement and adhesive were first treated as pigment.

'Then Bonamini enquired into the hardening process of the material, working on it with an incision of constant form and pressure,' he wrote. 'The outcome was a succession of scratches which tended to disappear as the drying process was completed. The variation of the adhesives signified a different behaviour on the material: a matter of wishing to associate the constant differentiated reaction of the cement in the face of the same aggressive process.

'This was the reasoning on the "relativity" of the means and on the outcome which was accepted on its merits as a direct and true testimony of the working process. One must, together with this, look at a further enquiry made by Bonamini into materials in about 1977 when the scratch on the cement was replaced by ribbons of canvas soaked in different strengths of peroxide and, successively, placed in ink for a constant time. The result – each strip corresponds to a specific degree of absorption of the ink – becomes part of a sequence in which the various elements are displayed in succession, evidencing in its horizontal layout, the diversity of the physical results in the presence of the identity of the gestures.'

To those not familiar with the language of abstract art the above may certainly seem esoteric, but art depends on innovation if it is not to decline. The great artists of the 20th century all added to the progress of art by experimentation. And how successful has Eros Bonamini been in his development of new modes of expression related to his 'curiosity on the operation of time'?

In the introduction to "Cronotopografie" the art critic Eugenio Miccini declared, 'I have known very few artists of such clear intelligence and equally vivacious irony. For the past twenty years he has continued to develop constantly and coherently his research, by finding himself out of step with certain of today's artistic expressions.' And the art expert Giorgio Cortenova has written, 'Following all his works over the years... I feel it fair to state that it is rare for an artist of our time to be able coherently to renew and enrich his work as does Bonamini. What is more, I cannot hide the intense feelings I have, the sensation his work gives me.'

It is not just the words of art critics that endorse his work but the large number of exhibitions around the world in which it has appeared. While he proclaims his ideas in abstract art he also paints still lifes and landscapes.

His work, that some call avant-garde, is an example of how members of the MFPA develop their own styles. There are over six hundred such artists in the world and they have over six hundred approaches to art.

Eros Bonamini the artist is famous, Eros Bonamini the man is reserved when it comes to speaking about himself. To the author he did go so far as to say, 'I love to travel a lot, I love many things... I am married and my wife is called Giuseppina, at home we call her "Giusi", and my parents in their own house are not far from our home.

'I have no religious conviction though I have a religious culture having been educated in a certain way but I am very logical – absolutely logical! – and to someone who has had my kind of experience in life I would say that culture is an option and can become a reason for living.'

In 1992 Eros Bonamini joined the board of the MFPA and ten years later was elected President of the Association worldwide.

Jolanta Borek-Unikowska

'The world of imagination saved me.'

It is bad enough for a person to discover that they are suffering from a mysterious debilitating ailment, but to be ashamed of the fact makes it doubly distressing. This was the situation that twelve-year-old Jolanta Borek-Unikowska found herself in when she found it increasingly difficult to keep up with her brothers and sisters. She tried to hide her loss of energy and spent a lot of time sitting in a chair pretending to read or sew so that her family would not guess there was anything wrong with her.

The reason that Jolanta says she felt ashamed was that she was desperate not to be a burden on her family, especially her father. Shortly before Jolanta had become aware that there was something going wrong with her body her beloved mother had died leaving six children.

At first it was thought that their father would not be able to cope with such a young family but he proved to be a rather remarkable man. Somehow he managed to run the household and continue to make his living.

'He looked after us carefully and for that we will be grateful to him until the end of our lives,' says Jolanta.

Jolanta had been born in Nowogard, Poland, in 1948. When she was six her family moved to Szczecin where she attended primary school with her brothers and sisters, and where she lives today.

Looking back on her early days she recalls that when their father took charge of domestic arrangements her home became a 'bit different' to those of her friends.

'We did not clean the house on Saturdays and cook cakes as other girls did,' she says. 'We used to drink tea and have discussions with my father who was an amateur historian and violinist, and who made sure that each of us had a hobby; I was very keen on painting. We all played chess, and afternoon tea was an everyday ritual.'

The time came when Jolanta found it more and more difficult to hide her ailment. She tried to climb the stairs when there was no one around to see how difficult she found it to haul herself from step to step, but before long her secret was out. A doctor was called in and after tests were carried out his diagnosis was that Jolanta was suffering from muscular dystrophy, a disease which progressively weakens the victim and for which there is no cure.

Now that she knew the worst, Jolanta was determined to make the best of her life. She managed to continue her schooling and after college she hoped to attend an art school – it was her dream to become a fashion designer.

'When they found out that I suffered from such a serious and progressive disease they refused to give me a place,' Jolanta says.

Her father suggested that she studied to get a profession but one day she woke up to find that she could not use her arms. To add to her distress her beloved father, who had seemed to be 'an indestructible man', died in 1982 and her world collapsed.

As Jolanta explains, 'It was the beginning of a long and deep depression, made worse two years later by the death of my sister who had looked after me after Father's death. The world of imagination saved me. I was dreaming most of the time, dreaming that I was painting. People and faces kept coming before my inner eye. They were happy and smiling – only one face was sad.'

Confined to a wheelchair and dependent on members of her family for all her needs, Jolanta's future seemed bleak and held nothing but the worsening of her condition.

If only she could paint! If only she could put on canvas the pictures that formed in her imagination! But such a notion was impossible. How could one paint when one's hands refused to obey her slightest command?

At that time Jolanta says 'Society wasn't so tolerant towards disabled people as it is today. I could not go anywhere because there were no facilities for wheelchairs and so I did not go out for twelve years.'

Then one day in 1994 Jolanta was watching television, her window on the outside world, when she learned of the inauguration of The Foundation for Helping People with Muscular Diseases. She wrote to the new society explaining her situation and after an official visited her she was offered a 'rehabilitation holiday' in the beautiful resort of Wagrowiec.

'It was the first time I had been out since 1982 and there I met wonderful people – people who were disabled like me – with whom I felt a bond of companionship,' Jolanta says. 'There I met an artist named Andrzej Grzelakowski – known to his friends by the nickname of Aga – and when he found out that I had a deep interest in painting he invited me to a painting workshop he was holding in a studio by Wagrowiec's lake.'

It was there that Aga set out to convince Jolanta that it would be possible for her to paint by holding a brush in her mouth. At first it seemed impossible but the desire to put colour on canvas was so strong that she tried the technique and to her joy she found that she was able to control her brush by movements of her head. Her first proper picture was that of a peacock.

'That painting was very important to me,' Jolanta told the author. 'It symbolized the metamorphosis of my life. With tears of joy I started a new life...'

The artist Aga continued to teach his willing pupil and was delighted at the speed with which she learned the necessary techniques of using a mouth-held brush. When he felt she was proficient enough he sent some of her paintings to the Association of Mouth and Foot Painting Artists. In September 1995 the Association granted her a scholarship and her career as an artist was assured.

Since then Jolanta has happily devoted her life to art, working in a studio in the house on the outskirts of Szczecin where she now lives. In the studio everything is so organized that she can manage to work without help. Brushes and paints are arranged by her easel so that she can easily select what she needs by mouth. She works at her canvas for long periods at a time and is so meticulous that it sometimes takes her several weeks to complete one painting. Many of her paintings have been sold and she has had a highly successful exhibition of her work in Szczecin's Presidential Gallery. Jolanta's favourite subjects reflect the natural world, flowers, birds, trees and still life, and she is also known for her imaginative portraits of girls.

'Painting is psychotherapy for me,' she says. 'In the old days I had to take medicines, now I paint. Painting gives me peace and joy. When I am painting I forget the world and my disease is no longer a punishment.'

Apart from her artwork Jolanta is the chairperson of The Foundation for Helping Children Suffering from Muscular Dystrophy and she also organizes seminars for disabled children.

Shih-Feng Chen

'As long as you don't give up you'll reach your goal.'

It was a warm summer day in 1996 and in an elementary school in Taiwan the pupils pined for the open air but in one classroom their restlessness changed to dutiful respect when the head teacher walked in holding a new book in her hand.

'I have read something that is quite amazing,' she said. 'And now I am going to read it to you and I want you to think about it because there is a great deal you can learn from it.' There was a universal sigh. This sounded boring.

'It is the story of a boy who could have been one of you,' the teacher continued. 'Something dreadful happened to him but in end he has become a hero. I hope he will be an example to you all.'

This sounded better. There were looks of expectation on the young faces as the teacher opened the book and said, 'His name is Shih-Feng Chen...'

Shih-Feng Chen was born into an affectionate and fun-loving family on 19 March 1969. His father was able to provide adequately for his five children thanks to his employment in a local steel mill while his mother enjoyed her role of housewife, to use what is now a politically incorrect designation. Thus the boy entered a happy childhood, played games with his brothers, started school and enjoyed the security of a stable home life.

Sadly this was to take a drastic turn when one day a grave Mr Chen told his children, 'You know that your mother has been unwell. I am sorry that after the tests she has had, the doctors say she's really ill. They told me it is cancer.'

As his mother's condition deteriorated the joy went out of Shih-Feng's life, and he felt his world had ended when she died not long after his tenth birthday. In the days that followed her funeral Mr Chen decided that if he continued going to work each day he could not look after his children adequately. Being a man of resource he decided to resign from the steel mill and start a small workshop in the backyard of their house. This way he was able to continue to earn a living and be there for his children. Conscious of the effect of their mother's death upon them, he became lenient in his parental control and this, combined with the shock of his bereavement, led to Shih-Feng becoming rebellious.

By the time he was fourteen his bad behaviour was a great worry to his father who, hoping to keep him at home and out of trouble, gave him a young pigeon to raise. The boy was delighted with his pet. As the bird grew he decided to fix a flag at a second storey window so that when it was flying free he would be able to recognize the entry to his home. The boy leaned out of the window, reached down... and the world went black. He had accidentally grasped an electric cable.

When Shih-Feng regained consciousness he found he was in a hospital room. As he drifted between awareness and sleep he heard enough hushed conversation to understand that as a result of being electrocuted his arms were paralysed. It also became apparent that his family was dissatisfied with the medical treatment he was receiving and were praying for some solution to their concern. The answer came when word reached them of a 'miracle doctor' who was noted for his treatment of similar cases at his clinic in Kao Hsiung.

A week after his accident Shih-Feng was in the care of the new doctor who, after giving him an intensive examination, had a private conversation with Mr Chen. When Mr Chen returned to his son's bedside there were tears in his eyes. He knew what lay ahead for the boy.

For the next three months Shih-Feng was in constant pain from the series of operations that were performed upon him yet such was the care he received it was not until he was home again that he realized the full extent of his disability. He could still walk but having had his hands amputated, and with his arms without movement, everyday life presented countless difficulties.

It was at this point that Shih-Feng decided to fight back against fate. He might not be able to hold his pen any more but this did not stop him learning to write by gripping it between his teeth. His arms might be useless but this did not stop him cycling. He could not control his direction by holding the handlebars of his machine but he could by the movement of his body. Then, in 1987, his interest in art was awakened and he began to experiment with oil paints using a mouth-held brush.

Seeing the effect of the pigment on canvas fired his ambition to become an artist and from then on he dedicated himself to mastering the techniques of his new craft. It became obvious that he had within him a hidden talent for painting, a talent that would probably have remained dormant if it had not been for that day when he leaned out of a window with his pigeon's flag. After a year of intensely hard work he felt confident enough to submit samples of his work to the Association of Mouth and Foot Painting Artists and was subsequently granted a scholarship to develop his talent. The Millennium year of 2000 gained extra significance for him when he was informed that he had achieved associate membership.

By now Shih-Feng was not only painting in oils but had also begun to use ink and watercolours to produce typically Asian motifs, which understandably were very popular in Taiwan at his first solo art exhibition held in 2001. Oil paints he reserves for his 'western-style' works, which include many still life studies of flowers notable for their rich colouring. Such studies are particularly suitable for the type of greeting cards produced by the MFPA.

Media interest grew in the artist without hands not only for his talent as a painter but for the determination with which he overcame his disability epitomized in his often repeated remark, 'As long as you don't give up you'll reach your goal.' Apart from becoming a professional artist, Shih-Feng has reached other goals he set himself. For example, after his marriage he was eager to take his wife out and about and to this end he learned to drive a car.

A history of Shih-Feng's 'indomitable spirit' in succeeding against the odds has been published in school textbooks to serve as a model for Taiwanese children.

Ruth Christensen

'One gains strength from having to struggle.'

When the Council of Europe decided to hold a competition for a mouth or foot painter to design its official Christmas card, hundreds of thousands of people around the world realized that 'art without hands' was not only possible but also highly professional. The card that was chosen out of the large number of entries depicted a snow scene with a group of happy children in Santa Claus dress pulling their sledge on which were lettered building blocks spelling out 'Europa-Europe'. It was the work of the mouth painter Ruth Christensen who over the years has become famous for her vivid pictures.

Ruth was born in 1929 at Lynge in Nordsjälland, Denmark. With four brothers and a sister she found life to be very cheerful and she looked forward to growing up when, she assured everyone, she would become an artist. One day shortly after her eleventh birthday she pedalled her bicycle on to a level crossing notorious for its poor visibility, had a fleeting impression of a locomotive looming above her and then merciful oblivion. Today she still has no memory of the actual accident, only of coming round in a hospital bed to discover that both her arms had been severed above the elbow. It was the beginning of her long fight to regain life's normal expectations, which seemed to have ended on the railway line.

'You can imagine how my accident cast a shadow over all our lives that up until then had been so carefree,' says Ruth today. 'That was one of the reasons why, when I came out of hospital, I was determined to get back to as normal a life as possible. I really strove to manage with everyday things, and gradually I began to succeed.

'I used my mouth to put on my doll's clothes, turn the pages of my book and I tried to write holding a pen in my teeth which was far from easy. The good thing was that I was able to keep going to my usual school. My father made an appliance which, attached to what remained of my upper arms, enabled me to use a fork so that I was no longer dependent on someone feeding me. It was a hard struggle but one gains strength from having to struggle like I did.'

This was proved when Ruth held to her ambition to become an artist despite its seeming impossibility now that she was so disabled. After she completed her school course she was disappointed by the response she received when she applied to be enrolled in an art school in Copenhagen. She was told, 'It would be far too difficult for someone without hands.'

Ruth refused to accept this decision, and after demanding to give a demonstration of her ability to draw with mouth-held pencils she was accepted. She commuted by train to Copenhagen for her lessons until the family moved to the capital, buying a house in the Vanlîse suburb where Ruth lives today.

After completing art college, Ruth's standard of work was so high she was able to get her work into various advertising agencies.

'I did all sorts of work; brochures, catalogues and advertisements, and I created designs for a linen manufacturer,' she recalls. 'It seemed that I had got over my handicap in that I was living a more active life than most. In 1960 I went to Canada to work in an advertising agency in Montreal.'

It was to be one of the most exciting periods in her life. Ruth learned more and more about artwork, was surrounded by friends with whom she travelled to the USA, and met her future husband. Their wedding took place in Copenhagen in 1964.

The couple settled in Nordsjälland where, to Ruth's huge delight, her son Thomas was born. She continued to freelance as an advertising artist, which was to be of great benefit when the marriage ended after nine years. Ruth returned to Copenhagen with Thomas where she moved into the upper storey of her parents' house. Here she had a studio for her freelance work but now as a single mother she found life was difficult financially.

A milestone in her career came when the Danish branch of the Association of Mouth and Foot Painting Artists heard about her work and offered her a scholarship. In 1982 she became a full member of the Association and in the same year one of her paintings was chosen for a Christmas stamp by the Royal Danish Post.

'To become a member of such a partnership as the MFPA and receive a regular income was a marvellous lifting of my problems,' Ruth explains. 'It has made it possible for me to develop my own style as it was always my ambition to do. Working in my own way gives me freedom. When it came to painting in the beginning I wanted to do everything correctly; to paint everything exactly the way it looked, but as I learned more I dared to go my own way. I get ideas from actual things and like to go around with my sketchpad, and when I get back to my studio I look at my sketches and let my imagination have full rein. When I decide what to do I make a drawing on the canvas, begin to apply the colours and then the painting goes its own way. It is as though something takes over.

'Although I like to work with watercolours best I find that by switching to different mediums and trying new techniques I do not get stale. For this reason I try to use oil paints sometimes but I find the pigment heavy. When I do use oils I do so as if they are watercolours, applying them in thin transparent layers which are easy to work over.'

One motif that has long fascinated Ruth is that of a flower in a glass vase with light streaming through it and a view of a room behind distorted by light refraction. It is one of the hardest subjects for an artist to tackle but she has returned to it many times.

The many greeting cards that Ruth has painted are not only known in Scandinavia but are published internationally. She believes that a key to their success is the fact that she has worked as an advertising artist, the message of her cards is direct and people respond to it immediately.

Looking back on her life Ruth admits that she has 'had it good'.

'Life is easier for me than most other members of the Association in that I can walk freely,' she says. 'I am able to use a car with the help of special steering equipment and in summer I spend time in a house on the coast which charges my batteries. I am also very lucky that I am on close terms with my family. Best of all is the fact that I have the opportunity to paint without economic pressure. It is painting that I want to continue with for as long as I am capable of working.'

Ruth is a dedicated worker on behalf of her fellow disabled artists, especially those in Scandinavia whom she represents after being elected an MFPA board member. Not only does she travel to the Association's headquarters twice a year to confer with other board members in the Association's "Parliament" but also, in company with her sister Lis, she tours the Nordic countries visiting fellow members to discuss their ideas and well-being.

Dennis Francesconi

'I grew tired of being known as "X".'

At seventeen years old Dennis Francesconi found life very much to his liking. Full of the robust health that comes with a love of the outdoors, his two greatest pleasures were taking part in sporting activities, which lately had included water-skiing, and working on his parents' Californian ranch. Then, as has happened with several other artists in this book, in a matter of seconds his life was irrevocably altered.

'On a hot summer day in 1980 I went on a family outing to a local reservoir to have a little fun skiing,' Dennis recalls. 'I was skiing around quite quickly when the boat made a sudden turn and started heading in the other direction while leaving me on my original course. Then I realized that if I hung on to the rope I would clip a small wooden structure as well as a few rocks. So I let go of the rope and cut to the right and within mere seconds my skis made contact with the sand.

'I was catapulted over thirty feet in distance approximately six feet off the ground and landed on my head. I flew right past my dad who was sitting on the tailgate of my truck. The next thing I heard following the impact was my mom screaming.

'Oddly enough, as the bones in my neck were crushed against my spinal cord I felt no pain. In fact I didn't even feel the rest of my body hit the ground. As I lay flat on my back looking towards the sky I soon realized that I could not move or feel anything below my shoulders. Paralysis still did not cross my mind because I knew nothing about it.

'Suddenly my dad appeared at my side and asked, "Are you OK?" After telling him that I could not move or feel anything he quickly instructed a friend to get an ambulance, and everyone else to stay back as he held my head steady. Obviously he knew more than I and suspected the worst.'

During the next eighteen critical days at the hospital Dennis's parents shared time there constantly. His father would sit in a chair in the corner of his room every night while his mother came during the day and did the same. That show of caring and devotion by his family, including that of his brother, is something that Dennis says he will never forget.

In the months that followed tests, evaluations, surgeries, and the words 'permanently paralysed' became part of his world.

Having been in hospital for slightly over three months had taken its toll. Sleepless nights and constant therapy brought pure exhaustion, and the realization that he was paralysed from the chest down, and would remain so, caused him to suffer the deepest depression.

'My whole world was turned upside down,' he recalls. 'I had never been a guy who could sit down and watch television. I always had to be doing something, whether it was working, playing sports, or some sort of recreational activity. Now I had to face up to having my hands paralysed and without feeling up to the elbows – not to mention the rest of my body. Human hands are a magnificent gift that all too often people take for granted. Look at the simple things, like petting my dog, tying my shoelace or combing my hair... all those things were gone.'

As Dennis put it, at that point he did not consider himself lucky, but when he saw other accident patients such as those with brain injuries he thought of how he had flown through the air and hit the ground, and how easily he could have been one of them. Then, and only then, he realized that he still had something to be thankful for.

'When I went home to the ranch in Madera, California, plenty of friends would come around but I was often depressed,' he says. 'I never really let it show because I did not want to appear weak. Up until then I had loved the ranch – I was made for it – but now I found there was nothing for me to do and I hated it.'

This life of frustration continued for two years and then everything changed – this time it was for the better. By chance Dennis met a charming and intelligent young woman named Kristi who he had not known prior to his accident.

In describing the effect she had on him, he has written: 'Truly a guardian angel of sorts, Kristi and I developed a relationship, a partnership, and together set out on a quest. A simplistic storybook journey it was not. Only after several long years of searching for some way to achieve and flourish did we find it.'

Kristi believed that if Dennis could find some employment it would help to restore his self-confidence. One of the jobs he tried was selling vitamins for a health product company but this was not a success as he explains with a grin, 'Potential customers looked at me as much to say, "*You* are trying to sell *me* vitamins? You hardly look a picture of health yourself!"

'Interestingly enough the breakthrough began with the need to write my name. I grew tired of being known as "X" so one day in an act of frustration I got a pen between my teeth and proceeded to write my name. I could not believe I had done it. So then I started writing down my thoughts and things like that, and while I wondered what to write next I would doodle. I started copying little things around the house just to kill time while I was thinking.

'Kristi started putting them on the refrigerator like I was a little kid bringing them home from school. They were 10-, 20-, 30-minute sketches and that's when I started thinking, "Hey, maybe I've got something." So I started doing sketches of an hour, two hours, five hours and more. I

was intrigued by it and each time they got better and better.'

Living close to Dennis was a disabled artist named Clayton Turner who was a member of the Association of Mouth and Foot Painting Artists. He took an interest in Dennis's work and suggested that if he concentrated on improving his technique and used colour instead of monochrome pencil or ink he should approach the Association.

'I worked on my technique for about two years and then got in contact with the Association,' says Dennis. 'In 1993 I completed roughly a dozen pieces in watercolour, submitted them to the MFPA and was accepted as a student right away.'

Not long after that Kristi said, 'We really should put a little more knowledge into our lives.' So she suggested that they both enrol at a local college.

'A lot of the classes we took together, the prerequisite things you have to take like English, writing, mathematics and so on,' Dennis says.

Despite the demands of the college, Dennis found time to paint for the Association and in 1996 he became an associate member. In 1999 he and Kristi graduated and Dennis says, 'I shall never forget our last day of college. Just before I was due to give a farewell lecture I received a letter informing me I had become a full member of by the Association. When I was wheeled into that class I felt I was about three feet off the ground.

'Membership within the Association has completely changed our lives. I had been on public support for many years, which was why we were always looking for a way to be independent. Thanks to the Association I don't receive one penny from the taxpayers of this country any more. We have reversed the roles – we pay taxes now and that makes us feel good.'

Talking about his work Dennis explains, 'I mainly paint from photographs. In the past my Dad took a lot of the photos, but Kristi takes most of them now. Watercolours are said to be the hardest medium to use but that's what I started with. Much of my work has been done in watercolour but now I'm moving to larger pieces on canvas I am using either acrylics or oils.'

His work is mainly representational but he also enjoys experimenting with abstract subjects because it gives him the opportunity to think and paint outside of the usual lines. On average he produces between twelve and fifteen paintings a year, each taking many hours. Indeed, he has been known to spend well over 150 hours on a single painting.

'As I see it, Kristi – my wife and my best friend – has been the catalyst in my life,' Dennis declares. 'If it wasn't for her, chances are I wouldn't be doing anything like this. There were things I was trying to learn for myself but she greatly enhanced my opportunities thus putting independence and success within reach. Her family has always been supportive as well. From day one they accepted me into their lives and never gave my condition a second thought.'

Looking back on his life Dennis adds, 'I believe God is everywhere and that everything happens for a reason. If you become disabled your senses are enhanced in another area but it is up to you to discover what that is. Maybe painting is a gift that God gave me. I think it is, and I'm truly grateful.'

DENNIS FRANCESCONI

Iwao Adachi
Celebration

Iwao Adachi   Castle Neuschwanstein, Bavaria

Eros Bonamini   Composition

Eros Bonamini   Market in Marrakech

134   ARTISTS WORLDWIDE

Jolanta Borek-Unikowska Lady in White with Pink Roses

Jolanta Borek-Unikowska Flowers in Blue Vase

Shih-Feng Chen Vase of Flowers

Shih-Feng Chen Country Village

Shih-Feng Chen Geese by the River

Shih-Feng Chen Sunflowers

Shih-Feng Chen Vases of Pink Flowers

ARTISTS WORLDWIDE

Ruth Christensen Sunset

Ruth Christensen African Child

Ruth Christensen
Rose Bouquet

Ruth Christensen
Christmas Compilation

Ruth Christensen Welcome

Ruth Christensen
Loving Animals

Ruth Christensen
Teddy Love

Dennis Francesconi
Bird of Paradise

Dennis Francesconi   A Delicate Balance

ARTISTS WORLDWIDE

Kun-Shan Hsieh Graceful

Kun-Shan Hsieh Feathered Friends

Kun-Shan Hsieh

'I owe so much to the loving care of my mother.'

'Suddenly I entered a world of my own,' says Kun-Shan Hsieh describing his feelings when he had learned to control his mouth-held paintbrush. 'All the loneliness, frustration and pain disappeared when I was painting.'

For seven years this young man had believed that his future held nothing more than frustration caused by severe disability. To pass the time he taught himself to 'doodle' with a pencil held in his mouth. His 'doodles' gradually became drawings and then the ambition to become a painter stirred within him. But he was well aware of the difference between sketching and being able to paint properly.

Kun-Shan was born in Taitung in eastern Taiwan in 1958. His parents were of poor peasant stock but their poverty – five family members shared one tiny apartment – in no way prevented the boy from enjoying a happy childhood. In due course he attended an elementary school and when he completed his basic education he regarded himself as lucky when he was taken on as a worker in a garment factory.

In 1972 excitement spread among the staff when the news came that they were going to be relocated in a new factory. Kun-Shan enthusiastically joined in the work of removing machinery from the old plant. It was a break in the dull routine of factory life and he was in high spirits as he stood on a truck helping to load heavy pieces of equipment. Grasping a piece of metal he lifted it on top of the pile, forgetting how high he was above the ground.

The metal touched a high voltage cable overhead and a devastating burst of electricity surged through it and the youth who was holding it. He collapsed unconscious and was rushed to hospital where doctors carried out drastic surgery in order to save his life. When he finally opened his eyes it was to find that his entire left arm had been amputated, as had three-quarters of his right arm and his right leg at the knee. No wonder neighbours shook their heads; a youth with only one limb left would be a terrible burden on those who were already hard pressed in the struggle for existence. In those days there were no training programmes to help someone so handicapped, no computers that could be worked with a mouthstick or electronically controlled wheelchairs.

'I owe so much to the loving care of my mother.'

These words have been repeated over and over by Kun-Shan when giving interviews to journalists about his art and life. Yet no matter how many times this phrase has been quoted it never loses its sincerity as far as he is concerned. He can never forget that after his accident a number of his relatives and family friends were full of suggestions as to how his parents could rid themselves of a severely disabled son who was not only a financial liability but required constant nursing. Perhaps a home for incurables...

Kun-Shan's mother's reply was to insist on keeping him at home with her regardless of the problems this would entail. Months passed as Kun-Shan slowly recovered from the surgery he had undergone and he continually asked himself what the future could hold for someone who had lost the use of their body and whose only ability was to use a mouth-held pencil. And as the months became years the question remained unanswered.

Life took a turn for the better for Kun-Shan in 1980 when a professional painter showed him the techniques of oil painting. From then on he practised for ten hours a day and often he became so exhausted he fell asleep in front of his canvas.

When he felt confident that he could control his mouth-held brush he attended art classes to learn the essentials of what was to be his unexpected profession. As his technique improved word began to spread about this young artist. In 1985, when he held his first one-man exhibition in Taipei, the leading Taiwan artist Shiuan-shan Wu told the Press, 'He is fast becoming one of the best in his generation. There is a special touch of humanity in his paintings.'

Reuter's correspondent covered the exhibition for the media outside Taiwan with the result that an article about Kun-Shan appeared in "Reader's Digest".

'In a country still primarily interested in Chinese watercolours and calligraphy, Hsieh's paintings have created a new interest in oils,' the "Digest" declared. It also quoted Chau-chu Ho, a committee member of the Taiwan Oil Painting Association, who in speaking of Kun-Shan, stated, 'He has set an example to all the handicapped that they are not a burden on society but rather a creative force if they are given the opportunity.'

The article came to the notice of the Association of Mouth and Foot Painting Artists with the result he was invited to join and in 1990 he became a full member. Seven years later he won the American visual arts prize of the Association for Especially Talented Artists. Since then his reputation has continued to grow and in 2002 he wrote his autobiography under the title of "I am Kun-Shan Hsieh", which achieved great success in Taiwan and has been translated into several languages.

What is intriguing about his work is the fact that he is at ease with both European and traditional Chinese techniques. His favourite motifs are flowers and animals and a typical example of his traditional work shows a pair of birds with bright plumage amid the most delicately tinted blooms. In contrast a picture with a European influence depicts flowers in blue flower pots painted with bold impressionistic strokes and gaudy colours that seem to radiate sunshine and heat. It seems remarkable that two such differing paintings could be the work of the same artist.

In speaking about his work Kun-Shan declares that he still wants to learn more about painting and that it is his aim to establish a unique style of his own that will reflect in his works.

Apart from giving Kun-Shan a profession, his involvement in art led indirectly to the happiest aspect of his life. In 1980, when his interest in painting had begun to change his life, he visited a friend at his studio near Taipei. Here he met a charming girl named Su-Fen Line and was greatly attracted to her. In 1987 they were married and today they have two daughters, Ning who was born in 1989 and Hsuen who was born in 1992. One of Kun-Shan's chief delights is to go swimming with his daughters.

Apart from painting and his family, his greatest enjoyment is in travel and his other interests include Chinese chess, watching ball games and singing; a full life for one who once believed he had nothing to look forward to.

Thomas Kahlau

'I had found a way to express my pain.'

It was a bright June day in 1976 in Potsdam. To fifteen-year-old Thomas it seemed that all was well in his world. Exams were over, summer holidays were only a week away and he had set out on his bicycle to go swimming with his friends Olaf, Thorsten and Jörg.

When they arrived at the gravel-pit 'lake' they passed a green Soviet Army ambulance parked in the shade of the forest trees, Potsdam then being part of the German Democratic Republic. The boys hurried to a stretch of water which was divided by a small promontory.

'We can jump from that,' someone shouted. They undressed, they checked the depth of the water for diving, then one after another plunged joyfully in. But when Thomas made his second dive he realized something was wrong. Having entered the water at too sharp an angle, he shot straight down until his forehead struck the gravel bottom.

When he floated up to the surface he attempted to move his body but it failed to respond. His friends jeered at him in a friendly fashion, then Olaf cried in alarm, 'He's all blue in the face!'

The boys managed to lift him ashore and one raced to get help – thank God for the Soviet ambulance!

In his autobiography "Die Kraft in Mir" ("The Strength in Me") Thomas described what happened next.

'The trees, the bushes, the sky – everything looked so different, so strange,' he wrote. 'Then I heard Russian words. I was put on a stretcher. Treetops were dancing in the blue sky. A hand hit me in the face but it was my own hand. I could clearly feel it on my face yet I could feel absolutely nothing in my hand...'

He was rushed to the intensive care unit of the Potsdam Hospital where sometime later his parents and sister were told that due to injury to his spinal cord he would remain a paraplegic for the rest of his life.

Soon after Christmas he was transferred to a rehabilitation centre for paraplegia at Sülzhayn in the border area of the Federal Republic of Germany. To go there he was required to have official permission, and the daily visits of his parents were no longer possible as they had to wait for the permits that would enable them to cross the border to see him from time to time. This understandably had a distressing effect upon him as their loving concern had been a great support during the bleak days that followed his accident.

Thomas's autobiography is a remarkably frank description of what it means to be suddenly paralysed, the sense of helplessness that follows, the long periods of black despair and the attempts to try and make something out of what seems to be a blighted life.

Today Thomas Kahlau is famous as a painter. He has won his independence and a renewed zest for living, a full-length film has been made of his life and the success of his artistic career was underlined when, in October 2000, the President of Germany awarded him the German Distinguished Cross in recognition of his artistic achievements and his social commitment. But he had a long struggle ahead of him before he overcame his adversities, both physical and mental.

Nine months after his accident he graduated to sitting in a wheelchair, until then he had only been able to see things from a recumbent position. But his elation was dampened when his mother next visited him and saw him in a wheelchair for the first time. He had expected it to be a happy surprise for her, instead tears ran down her face and her body shook with sobs.

'I should have known,' Thomas wrote later. 'It seems that only then she could understand the significance of what had happened to me. Before I had been ill to her – now I was paralysed.'

In December 1977 Thomas returned home, leaving Sülzhayn and 'the safe bosom of the rehabilitation centre' for good.

As with other people suffering from disability Thomas found that with the satisfaction of being back in the parental home there can be an element of stress for those who had to look after someone unable to do anything for themselves.

In "Die Kraft in Mir" he wrote: 'For me and first of all for my mother (a kindergarten teacher) it would, of course, have been best if she could have left her job. However, we couldn't afford it because of the low income of our family and my expensive care. At that time we had problems to make it from one salary to the next. So we tried to convince the district rehabilitation department that my mother, when she stayed at home, would get financial help for my care. However... they said there was no legal basis so Mother had to rush to work at midday, which was very hard for her because of the double load.

'As a result there were often tensions in our family and quarrels between Mother and Father about little things, the causes of which were obviously stress. And if, in addition, I was also in a bad mood – which was often the case due to my dissatisfaction – then my mother had to endure a lot. Sometimes I took all my frustration out on her and was very unjust towards her.'

Thomas's father was an inventive man and he devised an angled writing board with a small plate which when touched by the tip of a felt pen briefly activated a small electric motor with a relay and gearwheels. This caused a sheet of paper resting against the board to be pulled upwards for the space of a written line.

When the board was set up in front of Thomas a cigarette holder fitted with a felt pen was placed between his teeth. His first attempt was a scrawl but he tried again and successfully wrote his name, tapped his pen on the small plate, the motor whirred and wound the sheet of paper up for him to print on the next line.

'I didn't know how to thank my father,' Thomas wrote. 'I just accepted his help and this gift which would mark the starting point of my way to a meaningful life, making a basic commodity of it, which gave me back a little bit of my independence. It seemed that for my father this was the greatest reward for his efforts.'

Thomas now practised every day and in a very short time was able to write letters to friends and relatives. In those early days it took him about two hours to cover an A4 page with his large printing, today it takes him fifteen minutes to fill a page with 'joined up' writing which is very similar to his handwriting before his accident.

His mother gave him some writing paper which had a decorative cockatoo on it, and Thomas decided to copy it. More sketches followed and although drawing and later painting by mouth provided him with what might be termed a hobby, his main preoccupation was to find some manner of work by which he could earn some degree of independence. Almost by chance an answer came – to learn Japanese and become an interpreter.

In 1980 Thomas was introduced to an elderly Japanese gentleman named Mr Mainka who was a retired interpreter. Soon he was giving him weekly two-hour lessons in Japanese. Sadly for Thomas, Mr Mainka died after they had been working together for a year and the young man went into a period of depression. It seemed to him that he had not only lost a friend but his hopes of earning a living.

He wrote, 'The dream of a useful job which I would love was gone. I was paralysed and would never be able to do something useful. And I had thought that in my hopeless situation I could take up a career. Ridiculous. I would live off everyone and get on everyone's nerves and just

THOMAS KAHLAU

spend my life watching TV. There was nothing I felt like doing. When I finally forced myself to do something I just didn't seem to be able to do it properly... I painted pictures which I threw away afterwards.'

After a long period this negative mood ended and Thomas had his Japanese textbooks brought out again to resume a regime of self-education. His efforts were rewarded in 1986 when the Association of Interpreters accepted him as a member. Ten years after his accident he had earned a qualification and while he was delighted that at last he had a profession, another influence was developing in his life.

Knowing that his hobby was painting, friends and relations made a point of sending him cards and calendars whose pictures had been done by handicapped painters who like himself painted with mouth-held brushes. These he collected and the wish grew to make contact with some of these artists, to exchange ideas with those who had to face the same problems that beset him. Finally he wrote to the Association of Mouth and Foot Painting Artists in Liechtenstein. In reply he found to his surprise that it was possible to get a scholarship provided that his work was considered to be of a high enough potential.

Wanting to know more about the organization, Thomas contacted Reinhard Melzer, a mouth painter who suffered from cerebral palsy and the only MFPA member in East Germany at that time. At first he dimmed Thomas's high hopes by warning him of the very high standard of work that was required. But when he saw Thomas's paintings he was impressed and told him to submit them to the Association.

Thomas had doubts. Having a connection with a 'Western organization' was frowned upon by the East German authorities, nevertheless he set about painting five new pictures which he felt would be suitable for greeting cards; scenes of the Sanssouci Park in winter, a study of flowers and pictures of trees bent by the wind on the Baltic coast. They were completed in March and sent off. Thomas had done his best and now all he and his family could do was wait.

Time passed until he could no longer contain his impatience. He telephoned Liechtenstein in desperation, and to his joy was told that a letter was on the way informing him that 'thanks to his talent' he had been awarded a scholarship.

Apart from the fact that he would be able to have private tuition, it convinced him of his ability – drawing and painting was no longer a hobby but a career. Working harder than ever, he particularly enjoyed painting the landscapes of his native Brandenburg in oils, watercolour and acrylic. Under the aegis of the MFPA his work appeared in solo presentations in Germany and abroad and in 1995 he became a full member of the Association.

On the subject of his art Thomas says 'At first painting was a kind of therapy but as time passed I started to believe in the brushes and colours as though they were friends and trusted them... I had found a way to express my pain, my feelings, my emotions and thoughts. Painting became the most important part of my life. At last I could accept my unmovable body. And now the MFPA gives me the social safety I need for expressing my talent.'

Nancy Rae Litteral

'I couldn't have made it without God's love.'

The evening of 4 May 1954 in the small town of Wheelersburg in Ohio USA was warm and a fitting conclusion to what had been a delightful day. The senior class at the Wheelersburg High School was presenting a play and during the intermission the appreciative audience was entertained by the High School Sextette. The residents of Wheelersburg were very proud of the Sextette which had recently been televised in New York where it had come second in the Ted Mack Amateur Hour.

Among the Sextette singers was seventeen-year-old Nancy Rae Litteral who was looking forward to going to college in the autumn. The Christian faith was an important element in Nancy's life and her only regret was that her father, who had been religious as a young man, had ceased to attend church.

Looking back on that time, she was to say, 'I had enjoyed an ideal childhood along with an older sister, Anna Lou, and two younger brothers, Robert and David. With Mother we attended the Wheelersburg Baptist Church, and Anna Lou and I were going to go to the same college in the fall. Our whole life was ahead of us, we felt blessed.'

After the final applause Nancy was about to walk home, when friends offered to give her a ride to her house. Describing what happened next she recalls, 'On the way we were hit head-on by a drunken driver. The next thing I knew I was lying on the floor without movement or feeling. Later the hospital X-rays showed that my neck was broken.'

Members of Nancy's stunned family took it in turns to stay with her, hoping against hope that they would see her make some movement but she remained motionless. One night her father was sitting by her bedside when she asked him to read the 23rd Psalm. He took up a Bible and, when he finished the reading with the words '...and I will dwell in the house of the Lord for ever,' his daughter asked, 'Daddy, if I die will I see you in Heaven?'

It was too much for Ray Litteral. He had no answer and, unable to speak, left the room. Nancy then asked her nurse to call her pastor to tell him of the impact of her words and ask his help. As she recalled later, 'To my joy that night Daddy rededicated his life to the Lord. Our prayers were answered.'

Nine weeks after the accident Nancy's doctors had a meeting with her parents and told them that she would remain permanently paralysed from the neck down. As there was nothing further that could be done in the hospital it was suggested that she would be better off in her home surroundings.

Although this meant that she would be back with her supportive family, it was a dark period for the incapacitated girl. Looking back on that time, Nancy says, 'I went home, watched TV and cried. Instead of going off to college, here I was totally helpless with my parents taking care of me like a baby. I was full of self pity and questioning God, "Why me?"'

The mental darkness lightened when Nancy went to the Ohio State University Hospital for a year of rehabilitation. There she met fellow quadriplegics and out of their mutual encouragement came laughter. A device designed by occupational therapists made it possible for Nancy to hold a pen in her right hand, the only part of her body below her neck in which a tiny amount of movement remained. To pass the time that can hang so heavy on the disabled, she began "painting-by-numbers", putting colour into outlined spaces to build up a picture.

As a child at school she had been so inartistic she had bribed a schoolmate to do her art class drawings, but now she found to her amazement that she not only enjoyed this pastime but found she had some talent for it.

When Nancy returned from her rehabilitation course she found inspiration in certain Bible verses, one in particular being Philippians 4:13, 'I can do all things through Christ which strengtheneth me.'

'This verse showed me that I could live a life of paralysis for the rest of my life with Christ's help,' Nancy declares. 'I was fortunate to have such dedicated parents who sacrificed so much to care for me. We settled into a daily routine. After my mother and my father got me up in my wheelchair I'd paint until my arm got tired, then I would read, type – using a mouth-held stick to hit the keys – and watch a little TV before going to bed at eleven. We did this every day except Sunday when we went to church.'

Painting by numbers developed Nancy's ability to apply paint but after a while she wanted to be more creative and to this end she enrolled in a correspondence art course in 1960. She worked at this with dedication for the next three years. Her efforts were rewarded when she started to sell her paintings but then she began to suffer from an arthritic disease. It was impossible for her to continue to work with a brush fixed to her hand so she began to paint with a brush held in her mouth.

One of the problems that beset mouth painters is having to clench a brush handle between their teeth which can cause dental problems endangering the ability to paint. But in Nancy's case a dentist designed a holder that protected her teeth and allowed her to paint for hours at a time without discomfort. And so that she could select various brushes without having to keep calling to her mother for help, she used brushes with magnetic handles which enabled her to change them in the mouthpiece.

As her artwork improved her favourite subjects became still life, flowers and studies of children, particularly the latter. There is a poignant relationship between this and a remark of hers that was quoted in a magazine article, 'What I miss the most is to take a child into my arms.'

In 1979 "Reader's Digest" published an article on the Association of Mouth and Foot Painting Artists, and this fired her curiosity. She submitted several of her paintings to the Association for consideration but the reply was disappointing. The board did not consider that her work qualified her for a scholarship.

Some might have been downcast by the refusal or at least dismissed it with a mental shrug but not Nancy. At her special easel she worked harder than ever to get the pictorial effects that she wanted, and the following year she sent off another batch of paintings. This time she was accepted.

In 1991 Nancy's determination and hard work w rewarded when she was made a full member of the Association, and since then people in many countries have had the pleasure of seeing her work in the form of greeting cards.

Nancy once told the author that apart from work for the Association, she accepted commissions and a large part of her earnings from these is passed on to charities and to her brother Robert, a missionary in New Guinea, to be used to translate the Bible and to sponsor children in third world countries.

'I have an art show once a year and I enter my paintings in the county fair but most commissions come through word of mouth,' she says. 'I've painted helicopters, boats, cars, dogs and cats, and of course portraits of people's loved ones. Painting gives me much pleasure and a feeling of accomplishment. God has been good to me and blessed me with a wonderful supportive family, church and friends. I couldn't have made it without God's love or their help.

'We handicapped must not dwell on the things we cannot do but focus on the many things we can. Disabled does not mean unable.'

If Nancy's life could be summed up in a single sentence it would be in those last five words.

Anna-Liisa Lundström

'I can express in painting everything I want to say.'

'I was born a six-month-old foetus weighing only one kilo and spent the few next weeks in hospital in a kind of heated box with oxygen, but in spite of everything I decided to see what I could do for the world.'

With these deceptively light-hearted words Anna-Liisa Lundström describes her birth in Helsinki in 1952. Her anxious mother and father felt reassured as the weight of their tiny daughter began to improve but their happiness was tempered by the doctors' warning of possible complications, a warning that was confirmed when cerebral palsy was diagnosed as a result of her difficult birth. This physical condition made it impossible for her to co-ordinate her limbs. At the age of eight she was sent to a special learning centre in Solakallio where she was taught to read and count. When it came to writing the only way she could control a pencil was to hold it in her mouth.

As she grew older she began to show an interest in art.

'This came as no surprise to my parents as there were a number of artists in our family; photographers as well as painters,' says Anna-Liisa.

Showing an interest was one thing, to endeavour to paint with a mouth-held brush was another. Her first efforts with watercolours were far from successful as the colours dribbled down the paper, indeed it was stipulated that she had to paint out in the yard as one of her spasms would cause brightly coloured water in which she had washed her brushes to spray in all directions. However, her attempts improved when she was given oil paints, as they were not fluid.

When Anna-Liisa was thirteen her grandfather made her a special easel which she found to be very helpful. This made her very proud and stimulated her growing ambition to become an artist when she grew up. This was encouraged by her sister's aspiration to become a potter, the two girls making youthful plans to work together one day with Anna-Liisa decorating the pots.

In 1965, the same year that Anna-Liisa was given her first easel, she underwent neurological surgery in the hope that her physical condition could be improved and during the next seven years she had a number of such operations. Later in life when she was asked if these operations which marked her teenage years had helped her, she was able to reply, 'Yes. It was easier to paint afterwards because my body was more relaxed.'

When she had recovered from the long series of operations she was able to start at a vocational school in Helsinki. The next few years were hard for her. Her work was interrupted when she had an operation performed on her neck, and a year was lost when she was unable to find a carer to help her. Yet her determination to succeed against the odds became apparent when she later told an interviewer, 'In the spring of 1984 I took the secondary education exam for the first time – and failed. The following autumn I tried again – and failed once more. After that I continued studying at home but in 1986 I had an operation on my right arm, and then my wrist, but I carried on studying.'

The following year her perseverance was rewarded when she passed a final exam.

'I then became a university student with my white student cap,' she says. 'But I had to have another operation, on my left arm this time. When this was over I started a sociology course. I found the subject fascinating because the first thing we studied was the effect of different colours on the mind.

'I also studied oil painting at a vocational school where I tried many techniques and found that oils suited me best. With these I can express in painting everything I want to say.'

Despite the surgical treatment Anna-Liisa received, she could still only paint by holding a brush in her mouth. Yet she had no doubt about what she wanted to do with her life although she was aware of the many difficulties to overcome before she could become a professional painter. She told herself that she had to become more skilful, and to this end she continued going to adult education courses and taking part in summer schools to improve her technique. Stark images of nature were her subjects which were inspired by numerous visits to woodlands. Her impressions were transferred to canvas with strong colours which captured the light that gives a magical element to the Scandinavian landscape.

'Because the effect of light means so much to me the sea gives me exceptional inspiration,' she says. 'And because water and light are not far apart, water is found in almost all my pictures. It is easy to understand why Cézanne is my favourite painter.'

In 1989 Anna-Liisa's quest to become a professional painter took a step forward when the Association of Mouth and Foot Painting Artists took an interest in her work and granted her a scholarship.

'Meaningless work is over!' she cried when the news reached her. From then on her progress was steady and three years later she became an associate member. She took the opportunity to paint in Helsinki's famous Cable Factory, an old factory building converted into a centre where artists can rent studios.

In 1996, after years of hard work interspersed with frustrating periods when she was a hospital patient, Anna-Liisa achieved her goal by becoming a full member of the Association. In the same year she had her first public exhibition in Helsinki at the city's art gallery. Since then her pictures have been exhibited around the world. With her mother acting as her carer, Anna-Liisa enjoys a good social life in Helsinki, her favourite form of relaxation after a full day's work is to have a restaurant meal with friends. On average it takes her around fifty hours to paint a picture and usually she has three on the go so that she does not lose time while the paint dries on the canvas.

Discussing her work Anna-Liisa says, 'Personally I don't like still lifes, painting dead things. When I am about to begin a picture I am sometimes filled with a wonderful feeling about what the subject means to me and I can put the paint on the canvas immediately, otherwise I do a sketch first.

'Often pictures suggest themselves; they pop up out of nowhere, especially when I am relaxed. Perhaps it is the subject or the theme that makes me relax, for when I go into the countryside I feel my ideas undergoing a change. In summer I like to go to a cabin in the middle of Finland where I am in contact with the lakes and the forest.

'I feel I can express myself through my painting but I don't like to be described as someone who paints with a brush in her mouth. I would rather be judged by the same standards as normal painters.'

Serge Maudet

'I was born with a paintbrush in my mouth.'

'*Celui qui a fait mon costume est un bon tailleur*' is a typically French expression used by people happy with the way fate has treated them: 'The one who made my suit is a good tailor.'

It is a pronouncement frequently used by Serge Maudet though those who do not know him personally may wonder at his cheerful enthusiasm, for it seems the odds were against him when he was born in 1954 without the use of his limbs due to the rare paralysing disease known as arthrogryposis.

The Maudet family lived in the village of Roussay near Angers in France where Serge's father was a central heating engineer and his mother ran a chemist's shop. And it was his mother who encouraged him to hold a pencil in his mouth from a very early age so that childish scribbles would develop into writing.

'When I was a child I drew things I couldn't do, and then it became a way for me to express my feelings,' Serge explains today. He adds that the only time he was unhappy was when on medical advice he was sent to a special centre for disabled children in Paris. There, between the age of five and twelve he had thirty-five surgical operations in the hope of bringing flexibility to his joints. What upset him most was that the staff tried to make him use his ineffective hands to hold a pen. He found this to be impossible, to him the natural way was to use his mouth, and the conflict this provoked was so traumatic that he rebelled and refused to co-operate.

As a result of the operations his back was straightened to a degree and he was able to stand upright for short periods through he did not find this easy. However, he gained some movement in his legs so that today he is able to drive a specially adapted vehicle.

In between his operations Serge received primary schooling after which he returned home and started his secondary education, attending school with his brother. At the centre, Serge's companions were all handicapped so that disability seemed to be the norm, but to suddenly find himself surrounded by the able-bodied could have been an unnerving situation. It was probably his good humour that eased the situation for, as he says, 'I got on well with the others. They accepted me. But, of course, I could not go out and play with them in between classes so I stayed in the classroom – drawing.'

These periods when he was alone with a pencil and paper were the highlights of his day.

'Art was very important to me,' he says. 'My interest in it began when I was very young. I remember that the first book I read was about painters and Impressionism became my inspiration.'

His enthusiasm for drawing and painting, and perhaps making a career out of it, found no response with his teachers who told him, 'There is no future in art for handicapped people.' As he could write with a pen as well as draw, he was told that the only likely way he could earn a living was by becoming a book-keeper. His parents shared this view. After all, how many able-bodied art students were able to make profitable careers as professional painters once they had left college!

When he was seventeen, Serge dutifully embarked on a correspondence course in book-keeping but before long he realized that such an occupation was not for him. The lure of art was too strong and accepting this his father converted a garage into a studio for him; there was no doubt about his ability to draw, perhaps he could become a draughtsman.

When he was in his makeshift studio friends would congregate to watch him working at his easel and before long he was giving advice and lessons to other would-be painters. It was at this point that he visited an art exhibition at Angers where he met a remarkable lady named Denise Legrix and his career took a giant step forward.

Denise Legrix was born without arms and legs yet even as a child she found fulfilment through painting with a mouth-held brush which she later described in her autobiography "Born a Human", the proceeds of which went to a medical foundation. Her impressionistic paintings were exhibited widely in France and abroad and among the honours she received was that of being made a member of the Legion of Honour.

Impressed by Serge's work, she encouraged him to send examples of it to the Association of Mouth and Foot Painting Artists of which she was a member. After they had been evaluated he was given a scholarship and received private tuition from Professor Lise Driout in Paris.

From then on Serge's career with the Association progressed so well that in October 2002 he was elected a board member of the organization. This was particularly appropriate as over the years he had devoted a lot of time and effort to encouraging young would-be painters both disabled and able-bodied with lessons and workshops. Particularly popular are the annual summer courses that he organizes in Alsace.

At the same time he had concentrated on his own artistic output, his pictures having been exhibited in cities around the world, ranging from Sydney to Shanghai and Atlanta to Prague.

'Colours, shapes and perspective are my everyday companions, a necessity in my life,' Serge declares. 'When it comes to technique I like to try everything – pencil, chalk, charcoal, oils, gouache, ink applied with feathers – everything. Deep down I'm a painter, nothing else. When I'm in front of the canvas I don't think about my handicap. I was born with a paintbrush in my mouth!'

He endeavours to do as much outdoor painting as possible despite the difficulties that disabled artists encounter. When he sees a scene he wishes to paint his method is to make lots of quick sketches with notes on colour tones and lighting effects after which he is able to work on the picture back in his studio. These days he makes use of a digital camera to aid his memory.

From his marriage, which ended in separation, Serge has two daughters named Camille and Anaïs who, he says, take after their mother in their interest in music and after him in their interest in art. He has been quoted as saying with justifiable pride that they are his 'real reward' in life.

'The love and confidence of my family and of friends met along the way have enabled me to work out a certain philosophy,' he declares. 'There are only two ways of making your way through life – by crying or by smiling and accepting everything that comes. True grace is the grace of love.'

Cristóbal Moreno-Toledo

'All life is beautiful.'

For the first four years of his life Cristóbal Moreno-Toledo, who had been born in Córdoba in 1941, was like any other lively little Spanish boy. Then his parents became aware he was showing worrying physical symptoms. They took to him to a specialist who to their distress diagnosed progressive muscular dystrophy, the relatively rare disease which usually begins in childhood and continues to waste the victim's muscles for up to twenty years, leaving the affected areas without power of movement.

It was decided that the condition could be relieved by a series of surgical operations. Each time the child was admitted to hospital there was an upsurge of hope, only to be dashed when it became clear that the operation had not been a success. When the accelerating disease affected his legs it became necessary for him to use a wheelchair but for a while he retained the use of his arms. Using them to propel himself he was frequently seen racing in his wheelchair through Córdoba's winding streets in a way that could only be described as stylish. And style is something that he has retained down the years despite his disability.

Because of his weak condition which followed each operation, he was forced to spend lonely hours at home with the result that while his friends played football, he retired into the world of his imagination. Writing about him, the author Francisco Zueras said 'He used his time to develop his profound intellect.'

When Cristóbal reached the age of thirteen he had lost the use of his hands but this did not stop him from falling wildly in love with a schoolmistress and, eager to appreciate the things that were of importance to her, he developed a keen interest in literature. He found it to be something that had the power to take him away from the world of the wheelchair on wonderful flights of fancy. The books he read inspired him with the idea of becoming an author and he realized that the first requirement of a writer is to be able to physically write.

To this end he experimented with holding a pencil between his teeth and before long he mastered the technique. It then occurred to him that if he could write this way he could also draw and his artistic career began. He entered into this new pursuit with his usual enthusiasm, teaching himself to paint everyday objects and scenes of the gentle landscape that surrounds his town which is renowned for its beauty and the fact that the author Miguel de Cervantes used it as a background for his novel "Don Quixote". His ambition to be a writer had given way to his desire to be an artist.

Later he took a correspondence course in artwork and, when he felt confident in the techniques of painting, he developed a distinctive style by generously applying colours with a mouth-held spatula. It was while he was training himself to become an artist that Cristóbal struck up a friendship with a young man named Javier Criado who was to trigger a turning point in his life. The two shared many interests and one day in 1962 Javier excitedly told him about a journal known as "Artis-Muti", the official publication of an organization devoted to the promotion of severely disabled artists known as the Association of Mouth and Foot Painting Artists.

Prompted by his friend, Cristóbal sent some of his drawings to the Association's office in Madrid where they were immediately dispatched to the head office in Vaduz, Liechtenstein. In March he was awarded a scholarship and soon to his amazement and delight he received the news that he had been made a life member of the

Association. This meant that from now on he could concentrate on art without any financial worries.

As his paintings appeared in more exhibitions his work began to show Impressionist influences and from that time he has demonstrated his versatility as a painter. To look through a catalogue of his work one sees powerful studies of people who have come to life on his canvas, a beggar woman with her child, a reclining nude, a farmer riding his donkey, a late night procession... Then there are still life studies of fruit, fish laid out ready for the pot, and portraits which have a delicacy associated with crayons that are in contrast to his bold spatula-applied oils.

Turning from canvas and paper he created a series of mother-and-child studies on ceramic tiles. He has also ventured into the field of modernistic sculpture, designing fantastic figures out of pieces of metal welded together. As it is impossible for him to do such work with his useless hands he sits in his wheelchair while a technician cuts the metal to his directions.

In 1993 Cristóbal went to Rome where Pope John Paul II granted an audience to MFPA members in St Peter's Church. During the audience he presented the Pope with a large portrait he had painted of him and in return he was given a Papal plaque as a mark of esteem. Afterwards Marlyse Tovae, then President of

the Association, received a letter from a Vatican official, part of which read, '...may I kindly inform you that His Holiness has instructed me to convey to you sincere thanks... for the presentation of the painting by the Spanish artist Cristóbal Moreno-Toledo. From his heart the Holy Father prays to God to protect and assist you, the esteemed members of the MFPA and all those close to them.'

Cristóbal has received many distinctions in his own country, France and the USA. To be working at something one loves and to receive recognition for it is a great achievement for a man with no use in his limbs, yet it is not enough for this quietly spoken artist with the flowing hair and a goatee beard. There is also his art gallery.

In Castro del Rio stands a picturesque gateway with a tiled arch, wrought ironwork and a guardian statue of a figure in classical drapery. Beyond this is the gallery which Cristóbal set up for the purpose of exhibiting the work of little-known artists. He has also organized several drawing and painting courses for artists disabled like himself.

Cristóbal has come a long way since as a lonely boy he first put a pencil between his teeth but the spark of his creativity is as bright as ever. He is a man who obviously loves life and he sums up his credo with the words, 'All of life is beautiful.'

Cristóbal Moreno-Toledo at the Vatican presenting his portrait to the late Pope John Paul II, who held a private audience with the artits, whilst they were in Rome for an International MFPA meeting.

Professor Manuel Parreño

'For me, life is like a train...'

'I shall now announce the winner of the first prize in the school painting competition,' declared the art teacher. A hush fell on the school hall. There were a number of good young artists at the school and to win the annual art prize was considered a great honour by pupils and staff alike.

'The prize goes...' declared the teacher '...to Manuel Parreño Rivera.'

In the applause that followed eight-year-old Manuel felt a sudden glow of triumph which was reflected by the smiles of his family; he had proved that despite extreme disability he was able to hold his own in the world of the able-bodied.

Manuel had been born in Valverde del Camino in the province of Huelva, Spain, in 1938. When he was seven months old his parents, José and Dolores, became alarmed when he showed signs of acute illness and rushed him to a doctor. Soon it became clear that the baby was suffering from poliomyelitis, the disease that in those days that was known by the descriptive name of Infantile Paralysis and which, until the introduction of the Salk vaccine, was a parent's nightmare.

'My family were very affected by my illness,' Manuel recalls today. 'They did everything in their power to give me the best medical care. They regularly took me to Seville to undergo any relevant therapy which might halt the progress of such a terrible condition. After the disease had abated, and at the end of a long process of convalescence, I was able to regain mobility of my neck and left leg, leaving me with a 75% loss of power for life.'

As a young child Manuel began to use his feet with the same dexterity as ordinary children learn to use their hands. He became so proficient at using his toes as fingers that he could thread a needle, but it was using a pencil that he enjoyed most. He produced his first drawings when he was four years old, and as he grew older he felt that he had a vocation for painting.

'My childhood was like that of any other child,' Manuel says, 'I did my schoolwork like all the other children, although it is true that I was unable to avoid the curiosity felt by my school friends and teachers when they saw me working with my feet and which still allow me to perform any type of work; cutting wood with a saw, banging in nails with a hammer, writing with a pen.'

Manuel's family felt reassured at the way he was coping with his handicap, then in 1955 his sister Dolores, aged 13, died as the result of a cerebral haemorrhage. Like the rest of the family Manuel suffered from the shock of bereavement but he had agreed to have one of his paintings exhibited in the window of a business establishment and he felt he had to keep his word. The picture was put on display a month after Dolores's death.

When word spread that the picture had been painted by foot rather than by hand a journalist visited Manuel and wrote an extensive article for his paper on this seventeen-year-old who painted in such an unusual way. The story was picked up by other newspapers, the international magazines 'Life' and 'Foto', and a television channel in the United States. This surge of publicity convinced Manuel's parents that his future might lie the world of art and so he was enrolled in the School of Fine Art in Santa Isabel de Hungaria in Seville.

At the end of 1956 Manuel was surprised to receive a letter signed "A. E. Stegmann" offering him the possibility of becoming a member of the Association of Mouth and Foot Painting Artists.

After what Manuel describes as a 'searching examination', he became a full member in July 1957, thus becoming the founder member of the Spanish branch of the Association.

'As a result of this my paintings started being seen in many parts of the world,' Manuel says.

It was soon after this that an attractive young woman named Josefa Cejudo Ramirez came to his home to work as a housekeeper. Manuel got to know her and found her to be, in his own words, 'a young lady of great spiritual wealth and special humanitarian feelings'. In 1962 Manuel and Josefa were married and later had a daughter they named Rosa Maria.

Early in 1962 Manuel received a visitor at his home in Valverde del Camino who had travelled from Germany to meet him. In appearance his legs seemed too short for his robust body and his hands were tucked a little too neatly into the pockets of his jacket, but his most striking feature was his eyes which gleamed with determination tempered with good humour. It was Erich Stegmann, the President and founder of the Association that had given Manuel the status of a professional painter. His remarkable story is told elsewhere in this book.

The pleasure with which these two men – one who painted with his mouth, the other who painted with his foot – met and discussed art and the Association can be imagined. Understandably the hours they passed together remain one of Manuel's brightest memories.

The name Manuel Parreño Rivera was becoming increasingly well known in the art world through exhibitions and work done for the Association. In 1973 Manuel, with Josefa and their daughter, moved to Madrid where he set up a studio which soon became a place popular with celebrities, people who were well known through literature, politics, the cinema and the theatre.

In 1980 Manuel was appointed Professor of the Municipal School of Fine Art in Valverde del Camino. And as a professor he gives lectures on art in towns throughout Spain and in Spanish-speaking countries, but he still finds time to concentrate on what was most important to him artistically, namely his painting.

The year 1989 was an important one for Manuel. Firstly it was the year in which his grandson Manuel was born. Secondly in that year he was awarded the special "Popular Copé" prize for being amongst the ten most outstanding artists in the province of Huelva. Manuel had turned his life into a success story but more was yet to come. In 1995 at an MFPA congress in Vancouver he was elected as a member of the Association's governing board. Five years later he was appointed an honorary member of the eminent "Pontifica y Real Archicofradia de Nuestra Señor de la Soledad de la Porteria" in Las Palmas, the patron of which is Her Majesty Queen Sofia of Spain. This followed the consecration of one of his works for a local church.

Speaking about the work that he and artists disabled such as he undertake, Manuel declares, 'It must be understood that the fact that a painting has been done with the feet or the mouth is irrelevant. This should never influence one's perception of its merit. What really matters most is the work itself, not the means whereby it was created. Since it is the brain which controls all the exact and precise movements of mouth, hands and feet, it is surely the brain which is the true craftsman.

'For me, life is like a train which sets off as one draws one's first breath. We set off with an unknown destination and with no knowledge of how much distance we will travel. I hope my journey will be long because the longer the journey is, the more time I will have to create and to be productive.'

Previous Page:
Kun-Shan Hsieh
Still Life, Flowers in Vases

Kun-Shan Hsieh
Sunflowers

Kun-Shan Hsieh
Flowers in Vase

Thomas Kahlau
Autumn Walk

Thomas Kahlau Berlin Dome

ARTISTS WORLDWIDE

Thomas Kahlau Poppy Field

Thomas Kahlau Windy Day

Nancy Rae Litteral   Yellow Tulips

Nancy Rae Litteral
Summer Bouquet

Nancy Rae Litteral   Tulips in a Basket

ARTISTS WORLDWIDE

Anna-Liisa Lundström
Ice Dancer

Anna-Liisa Lundström
Gazing at the Sea

Anna-Liisa Lundström Sunset

Anna-Liisa Lundström Along the River

Serge Maudet   Contemplation

Serge Maudet   Landscape

Serge Maudet
Sunflowers

Serge Maudet
The Window Box

ARTISTS WORLDWIDE

Cristóbal Moreno-Toledo Notre Dame, Paris

Soon-Yi Oh
Birds on a Tree

Soon-Yi Oh Orchids in a Vase

Elias Raftopoulos

'Life is an odyssey.'

Elias Raftopoulos admits that as a little boy he was naughty. 'They would often find me on the roofs of the houses in our village by the sea,' he told the author. Today something of that 'little boy' mischievousness remains in his character. He may not be able to climb on roof-tops any more but one feels he would if he could, if only to get a different angle for a painting.

Painting is in Elias's blood. His father was a successful self-taught artist with independent ideas who at one time was put in gaol for his left-wing views, his mother was a dressmaker who, as we shall see, had a great understanding of human nature.

'My father taught me a great many things,' says Elias. 'Not only about painting but how to be a nice human being.'

Elias was born in Chania, Greece, in 1958, where he attended primary and secondary school. He was doing his military service in 1979 when, to his sorrow, his father died. In the same year he enrolled in the School of Fine Arts in Athens. His high hopes of following in his father's footsteps as a painter tragically ended with a motorcycle accident in August 1981. His neck was broken with the result that he was paralysed from the neck down.

Elias's mother, who was now living in Athens, took care of her son and did everything to combat the deep depression that enveloped him.

'My mother was a very intelligent woman,' Elias says. 'She taught me how to live in a wheelchair, she did everything she could to make me take an interest in life again and when she sensed how unhappy I was that my painting days were over, she would say, "Don't worry, you will paint again and one day you will be famous."

'I could not see how, although I had an idea that some disabled people painted with brushes held in their mouths because we got some cards...

'My mother tried to make the home comfortable for me and convenient for my wheelchair. She turned the living-room into a studio to encourage me to take up painting by the same method as that used by the artists who painted the cards. I know she felt angry when I said I could not paint again but she still kept saying, "Never give up."

'But the future seemed so black that I did not want to listen to my mother. I remember that one day I felt so angry at my situation I told my sister, who was four years younger than I, to collect all the drawings and paintings that I had done before my accident. When she had done so I ordered her to throw them into the garbage.'

It was a gesture that must have been disheartening to Elias's mother but she continued to leave paints out and brushes positioned so that it would be possible for him to pick up their handles with his teeth. And then one day her efforts bore fruit. Elias was alone in their apartment and suddenly the urge to put paint on canvas was upon him.

'I started to paint again for one reason – it was always in my blood to paint,' he explains. 'Since my accident I had the idea that life was no longer for me. I was very young but after those first years I began to think about painting as a man thinks about a woman. I was still in love with it. Alone that afternoon I picked up a brush in my mouth and began to paint an imaginary girl.'

Other paintings followed as Elias became more and more familiar with the technique and after two months the walls were covered with his paintings that his mother had pinned up.

'I realized I was back in life again and I was so happy,' Elias declares. Such was his re-found enthusiasm for painting that only a year later his pictures were included in an exhibition in the town where he had grown up. At this time he received advice and encouragement from another artist who also painted with a mouth-held brush and who became so convinced of the young man's talent that he had a video shot of him at work which he sent to the Association of Foot and Mouth Painting Artists. The response was to offer Elias a scholarship in 1988 and ten years later he became a full member while today he fulfils the role of a delegate, travelling regularly to attend the Association's board meetings.

'I am ever grateful to Erich Stegmann who founded the Association,' he says. 'It is thanks to him that people like me are able to lead satisfactory lives through our art all over the world. Most importantly, we are able to express ourselves. Truly Stegmann was one of the great men of the 20th century.'

Speaking about his painting today, Elias says, 'The best moment comes when it is just me and the painting. Then the world disappears. One of my favourite subjects is the nude figure. When I paint them I feel great respect for the human form and the best critiques I get for my nudes come from women.

'I am a religious person, being born into the Greek Orthodox Church which has a great tradition of religious painting. While I was never taught to paint in that style – I taught myself – I am sometimes inspired to paint a religious subject such as Jesus, Holy Mary or angels. People sometimes find it hard to understand that I feel the same respect for one of my nude studies as I do for a religious study when I am painting one, but I love all painting.'

Elias is also well-known for the landscapes he paints of his native country which he portrays in vivid Mediterranean colours. He uses oil paints and watercolours, and for his drawings he has an exceedingly fine brush to apply delicate lines of watercolour. Next to painting is his love of travel and he has visited many parts of the world to attend art exhibitions and to seek new inspiration.

'Life is an odyssey,' he declares. 'The most important thing is to travel. I do not mean just physically but also spiritually. I always want to learn, to visit new places and to meet new people with an open mind. Today I live in the town that I was born in but I am often away, travelling with the help of Diana who has not only been my helper over the past eight years but also a friend. Without her I could not do what I am doing now. Although I am able to paint, if I want a glass of water I cannot get it.'

ELIAS RAFTOPOULOS

Mai Ryan

'I just had to get on with it.'

Phoenix Park in Dublin is one of the world's most delightful city parks. Said to be the largest park within the environs of a city in Europe, it has something for everyone. For Mai Ryan it has forest and field which provide the natural beauty that she seeks to copy on to her canvases. Those who frequent Phoenix Park are used to see her travelling along woodland paths in her electric wheelchair, her fair hair bright in the sunlight and her eyes eager to find suitable scenes for her b...

... e residential ... vely named ... – which is ... here that ... made her

... ild on a ... e living ... grass

... ot far ... were ... after, ... and ... here

... at the age of ... ed to make nursing her career, no doubt because there had always been a caring aspect in her nature.

'I went to Dublin to train as a nurse,' she says. 'In the first four years I did my psychiatric training and then I began my "general" and qualified in Cashel which was my local town. I then wanted to do my "maternity" and it was arranged that I should begin it in Dublin in the following March.'

Looking forward to when she would learn another aspect of her career, Mai continued to work at the Cashel hospital until the time came to go to Dublin. Then, on the bitterly cold night of 12 January 1976, all her plans came to an abrupt end.

'Some friends and I were socializing at a house which we left by car at 2 o'clock in the morning,' she says. 'It was a frosty night and what made the road extra dangerous were the sugar beets that had fallen from lorries and had become frozen pulp on the surface. The car struck such a patch, went into a skid and we crashed into a tree. The next thing I knew was coming round in hospital, the hospital where I worked, the next day. And I found I could not move.'

All the occupants of the car were badly injured – the driver died in hospital – and in the impact Mai had suffered a broken neck. It was a C4/C5 break which meant paralysis from the neck down.

'After a period of rehabilitation I was told I could go home,' Mai says. 'My parents were still alive but they were not very well and were not able to cope; they could not come to terms with what had happened to me. So my brother and his wife invited me to live with them and it was a good life considering my physical situation. Each year I went with friends on holiday – wheelchair and all – mostly to Spain. And I learned to use a computer, pressing the keys with a stick held in my mouth.

'Then, in 1990 my brother's marriage split up, my sister-in-law left to go to Dublin and I could not stay on. For nine months I was in a nursing home, but although friends kept visiting me it was not satisfactory and finally in 1990 I got a room in this lovely home for the disabled, called Cuan Aoibheann in the grounds of St Mary's Hospital, Phoenix Park. I am very happy here. I suppose that with the trees and fields surrounding it I find it similar to living on a farm.'

Mai tells her story without emotion but behind her prosaic words is a story of determination to come to terms with her disability and find an outlet for the enthusiasm that she had felt for nursing. It was the casual words of a nurse that eventually lead to a new career. She told Mai that she was going to an art exhibition and that her boyfriend taught art.

'He could teach you – help to fill in your time,' she suggested.

'I had always been interested in art but I never found the time to do it,' Mai explains. 'I did take a couple of night classes but I never finished them. Something always got in the way; my studies or social life. But now I decided that here was an opportunity to take up painting seriously.'

For a year Mai received tutoring from this young man, not only learning about the craft of painting but the technique of painting with a brush held in her mouth. After that she felt she could continue alone; it was still a pastime to fill the day-long tedium that can afflict the badly handicapped.

Then in 1996, Mai's 'hobby' took on a new momentum. She was told that a special art course was being established at Dun Laoghaire for people with disabilities or who were disadvantaged. She applied and sent photographs of some of her paintings with the result she was one of the twenty who were accepted, being the only student who painted with a mouth-held brush. Lecturers from the National College of Art held classes and Mai says she learned a great deal there, so much so that after two years it was suggested that she should apply for a place in an art college.

'The idea of college seemed too overpowering for me,' Mai admits. 'However, I applied but was not accepted and I was quite satisfied with that. Instead I got a studio in Dublin through the course I had taken at Dun Laoghaire. It was arranged specially for people with disabilities and I went there three days a week but there were difficulties. The roads round it were cobblestoned and very narrow which made it difficult and even dangerous for a wheelchair.'

Over the years Mai had come to love painting more and more, and at the same time she became more and more proficient. As with other disabled people described in this book the very act of putting paint on canvas and creating a picture helped her to overlook the fact she was in a wheelchair. Although she needed most things to be done for her, here was something that she could do entirely herself. When painting, her canvas became a little world that was all her own.

Up until the year 2000 Mai regarded herself as an amateur painter but this changed when a friend received a MFPA greeting card. The friend rang up the Association and eagerly described Mai, her method of painting and the quality of her work. The Association is always on the lookout for suitable new students and it was not long before Mai's painting ability was assessed and she was invited to join.

Apart from the various advantages Mai gained in becoming part of this artistic co-operative, she found that she now had an outlet for her work. Now, when she had the necessary tubes of paint squeezed and her brushes laid out so that she could reach them by bending her head forward, she felt she was no longer a hobby painter but a professional.

In discussing her work Mai says, 'I feel you can't really be taught to paint, it is only done by constant practising. I found it hard to get the expression in people's faces so when I started I practised drawing faces every day of the week, faces that were older and faces that were younger. And I tried drawing any object. I would look down at my shoes and sketch them from this position or sketch my hat from that position, or I would sketch chairs and things like that.

'Today I like to paint landscapes, particularly Phoenix Park landscapes. I think as you get older you appreciate nature more and more, and so I go out in my wheelchair seeking suitable scenes to paint and when I find one I ask a friend to photograph it for me so that I can work on it back in my room. Of course I paint scenes suitable for greeting cards and I get ideas for such pictures from the wildlife in the park, the deer and squirrels and so on.'

Twice a week Mai goes to the National Art Gallery in Merion Square where she finds inspiration from the exhibitions and the lectures given by experts. Mai's other activity is completely different and she laughs when she explains that she is an "Avon Lady".

'I used to get Avon products and then some members of the staff began leaving their orders with me,' she says. 'Then someone said why didn't I go in for it properly so I rang up that number in the catalogue – the "Do you want to be a representative?" number – and an area manager came to visit me and thought it would be a good idea. Now I have a least a couple of hundred pounds worth of Avon products coming into my room each month and the profits go to the unit. Among the things I have bought for the use of the residents here is a karaoke machine and a bingo machine that displays the numbers.'

When Mai is asked about how she came to terms with her sudden incapacity she replies thoughtfully that she was always a religious person and this helped her greatly after the accident.

'The trouble was that I did not know how bad my injury was at the beginning,' she says. 'My parents were told that I would always be paralysed but they were too upset to tell me. I only gradually began to understand my situation and when I did finally know for certain that I would be paralysed for life I realized I just had to get on with it.' And with a smile she adds, 'I was given ten years to live and that was thirty years ago.'

Mai's religious belief is still a support. She has visited Lourdes on a number of occasions with a group and she has found great spiritual comfort in doing so.

'It helps you to resign yourself to your situation,' she declares.

Grant Sharman

'I wanted people to see what I had painted come off the canvas.'

'I felt I had been kicked in the teeth,' says Grant Sharman looking back on the day when six of his paintings were returned by the Association of Mouth and Foot Painting Artists as they were 'not suitable for their requirements'.

The rejection hurt Grant who had held high hopes of becoming proficient in painting and now those hopes had been dashed. It seemed there was only one thing he could do. So he turned back to his easel.

Grant, whose parents had emigrated from England in the late 'fifties, was born in 1961 but the story of his interest in art goes back to 6 July in 1977 when he took part in an inter-house Rugby match at King's College Boys' School in Auckland, New Zealand. Like his peers in a country that, to put it mildly, is obsessed with rugger, Grant loved the sport and on this winter day (July 'down under' is equivalent to an English February) he was enthusiastically playing as a tighthead prop when he was thrown out of the ruck. Filled with the excitement of the game he dived back into the ruck, his head became wedged between two players and then the ruck collapsed.

Those who are not familiar with Rugby parlance may be mystified by the terms 'ruck' and 'tighthead prop', suffice it to say that when the mass of players fell Grant felt, as he put it, 'as though the world had collapsed'. In fact the impact had resulted in his neck being broken.

An ambulance raced the stricken boy to the Middlemore Hospital which mercifully was only a mile away from the school. Here 'skull tongs' – 'Horrible things!' Grant declares – were fitted to his head to immobilize his neck which nine weeks later was operated on. Surgeons wound wire round the vertebra and grafted bone on to

each side and five weeks later he was taken to the new Otara Spinal Unit at Otahuhu where he was to reside for the next ten years. He was told that he would have to spend the rest of his life in a wheelchair as, apart from some limited movement in his arms though not his hands, he would remain a quadriplegic.

At the unit, where he was the first inmate, Grant managed to resume his education with the New Zealand Correspondence School. As an indebted ex-pupil, the author can testify to the support provided by this remarkable institution which was established to educate disabled children, or those who lived on farms too remote for them to attend school, by means of postal lessons and radio programmes.

When it came time for him to take his University Entrance exams in Physics and English, Grant was wheeled in front of a typewriter with a stick strapped to each useless hand. For the next six hours he laboriously tapped out his answers by the end of which time he felt sick with fatigue. He vowed never to go through such an ordeal again but he changed his mind when he was informed he had passed in his subjects and later he did a course on the History of Art and finally completed a paper on economics through Massey University.

This educational success was very gratifying but it did not solve the question that he could not avoid – what was he going to do with the rest of his life? It seemed there were few opportunities for someone as disabled as himself. Meanwhile, he had recovered his physical strength sufficiently to learn to drive a car specially equipped for a quadriplegic and this gave him a wonderful sense of freedom after five years of being confined to a wheelchair. At the unit a surgeon told him now that he could drive it might be possible for him to find a job. Grant did find a job, working two days a week as a receptionist for a wallpaper manufacturer. It was a post he was to hold for the next seven years.

'I was very nervous at first in my wheelchair but the job was a great turning point in my life,' he says. 'It was tremendous to be with people in an ordinary situation and it gave me confidence to do a lot of things. Until then I felt useless but now I had a job to do and I did it. I was particularly touched when the staff arranged a 21st birthday party for me at the office.'

Meanwhile Grant became friendly with a disabled artist named Bruce Hopkins who, as a member of the Association of the Mouth and Foot Painting Artists, suggested that he should try painting with a mouth-held brush. Grant protested that he would find it impossible. Bruce was renowned for his cheerful confidence and he told Grant, 'Just stick it in your mouth and away you go.' Grant did as he was told.

'It was a pathetic effort,' he admits. 'I just wanted to throw it away but Bruce was very persuasive and the next night I was attempting to paint again. This time there was the slightest improvement but more importantly I was enjoying it and decided to keep trying, greatly encouraged by Bruce and my mother and father. Later on Bruce suggested that I should submit six of my paintings to the Association.'

To Grant's bitter disappointment these samples were declined but the rejection sparked off his determination to do better. He changed his style of painting and when he was satisfied that he had improved he submitted another six pictures. The nervousness with which he awaited the Association's verdict made him realize how much he wished to become a member.

An envelope from the Association arrived in January 1981. When it was opened for him the letter inside offered him a scholarship which meant that painting materials and tuition would be provided for him.

'I was really proud to sign a contract as a student of the Association. It was only after I had done this that I saw the potential of art to give me my elusive independence. I had something to focus on, and I remember my father saying, "If you become a full member you will have an income guaranteed for life." And I thought, "There are not many people, able-bodied or disabled, that can happen to." And so I worked and worked.'

Yet try as he might, Grant did not make the progress he had hoped for. The two teachers he had for periods during the next five years did not take him in the direction he felt he should be following. As a result he remained mainly self-taught and he was haunted by disappointment over the lack of success that he wanted so much.

One day in 1986 Grant was working at his easel when he was aware that he was being observed by a lady with a halo of snow-white hair. She was a professional artist named Doreen Jones on a visit to the spinal unit, and after watching Grant for a while she moved on without making a comment.

'She came again and went away but on her third visit she said, "Can I help?"' Grant says. 'Thanks to her everything began to happen. It was like a diamond encrusted in rock and she broke away the chips. My paintings changed almost immediately, becoming more detailed and professional as she taught me nearly everything I know.

'I owe Doreen a lot of credit because she showed me how to tackle subjects I thought were nearly impossible; bush scenes, ships in full detail and other complicated subjects which was great because I wanted to be a painter who could paint realistically. I wanted people to see what I had painted come off the canvas.

'My breakthrough came when I painted an eagle. When I finished the picture it appeared as though it was about to fly out of the picture. As I looked at it I felt that at last I was getting somewhere in the art world. This feeling was endorsed in late 1987 when I received a letter to say that I had been accepted as a full member of the Association of Mouth and Foot Painting Artists. I shall never forget sitting in my room by myself and re-reading that letter and realizing that I had finally achieved something.'

Bruce Hopkins, who had done so much to encourage Grant in his art career, had died two years earlier and this meant he became the only full member of the MFPA in New Zealand although there were several students, some of whom were in the Otara Spinal Unit. Understandably this gave Grant a sense of responsibility which showed itself in his efforts to put New Zealand on the map as far as disabled artists were concerned. As a result their work was published in Australia, North America and various European countries.

When Grant became a professional painter he could not help feeling that he was not a natural artist and he pondered on what it was that had enabled him to become proficient enough to become an MFPA member.

Talking about that time he says, 'When I had my accident my housemaster rode in the ambulance with me to the hospital. After that he kept in touch and became like an elder brother. Then religion meant little to me but when he became converted I began to take an interest in it, too. In 1980 I became a Christian and I do believe that it had a great deal to do with my success.

'I became very impressed by a book I read by Joni Eareckson, an amazing artist, paralysed from the neck down after a diving accident, who travelled the world lecturing and singing. When she signed a painting she put the letters PTL beneath her signature; PTL sanding for "Praise the Lord". And I figure that He has a big hand in the way I paint and I put the same initials on my work.'

After he had lived in the spinal unit for ten years Grant was able to have a two-bedroomed cottage built to his own specification at the back of his parents' house in Papakura as a result of his becoming a full member of the MFPA. The doors were made wide enough for his wheelchair and the kitchen and the bathroom were designed specially for his use. His studio had very large windows so that for the first time he was able to work in what he termed 'splendid light'. Here he had the company of his parents, and here his friend Jenny Anderson, a nurse he had got to know in the spinal unit, put out his paints to help him prepare for art exhibitions.

Before long the Otara Spinal Unit contacted him with a request that he would go back two days a week to talk to patients newly admitted there. It was a request that Grant readily agreed to.

'If you have broken your neck or your back you have a lot of questions to ask,' Grant explains. 'An able-bodied person is not so plausible as someone in a wheelchair; when the session is over they don't get up and walk away, they wheel away.'

In 1993 Grant won the Bruce Hopkins Memorial Art Award. The painting he had entered depicted two young boys watching a game of Rugby football; an indication that Grant had not lost his interest in the game even though he had become disabled as a result of taking part in it.

'The award was established after Bruce's death and I was thrilled to win it especially as Bruce introduced me to mouth painting,' Grant said.

Grant continues to paint and lives with Jenny, now Mrs Sharman, in a house with a spacious studio they built on a ten-acre site in a rural setting. One of their greatest pleasures is when MFPA members from overseas pay them visits.

'It is a marvellous place in which to paint and live and we are very happy,' Grant declares. 'I think I am an incredibly lucky person. Of course there are times when I get a bit low, when things don't go right, but then I think how fortunate I am and I snap out of it. To me the great thing about being an artist is that we do spread some enjoyment and give to others instead of always receiving, and we do get to leave a bit of ourselves behind when we go.'

Phillip Swanepoel

'God gave me a talent for painting when I needed it most.'

It is sometimes said that if a person has met with some adversity in life he or she has 'drawn the short straw'. In the case of Phillip Swanepoel it could be said that he drew two short straws. Yet there was no hint of what lay ahead for him in his carefree boyhood days on a smallholding near Randfontein, 40 kilometres west of Johannesburg.

Born in 1944, he was the youngest of a family of four and he gained a love of nature through rambling at will through unspoiled countryside. In those days there were no electronic games, CDs or DVDs to occupy the hours of childhood, indeed Phillip's home did not have electricity. When he was not doing his share of household chores he found his fun in building soap-box carts out of scrap wood and acting as 'assistant grease monkey' for his two older brothers who were forever tinkering with their old jalopies to keep them running. In short it was an active and healthy life for a growing boy – until early one July morning in 1953.

'On the smallholding water had to be pumped from a borehole and it was my job on this specific morning to start the diesel pump,' Phillip says. 'Somehow my clothing got caught in the wheel of the pump and I was spun around. As I was slammed against the concrete floor my right arm was severed from my body. A farmworker discovered me in a pool of blood and alerted my parents.

'My father rushed me to hospital where I regained consciousness and realized that my arm was gone. I remained in hospital for two weeks and started doing things with my left hand so that when I went back to school a month after my accident I could write with it. I later discovered my family, especially my mother, suffered more trauma through the accident than I did.'

It was remarkable how nine-year-old Phillip adapted to the loss of his limb. At school he played Rugby and soccer and with his left hand he became a demon marble-player, winning so many marbles that he increased his pocket money by selling them. And having had to help his brothers in maintaining their decrepit vehicles, he became interested in things mechanical and actually built himself a bicycle out of bits and pieces.

'I remember inflating the tyres of my bicycle by holding the pump with the toes of my right foot against the spoke of the wheel and pumping with my left hand – excellent training for what was to come.'

When Phillip was eleven years old he graduated from riding a bicycle to clandestinely driving a car.

'My mother was hard of hearing so sometimes I could drive my brother's car in and out of the garage without her knowledge, and when she was away with friends I was able to test my driving skills without interference,' Phillip recalls. 'I knew my brother would never teach me so I stole his car from time to time.'

Phillip began to handle a car on the open road without the benefit of a driving licence when he reached the age of thirteen. He explains, 'By the beginning of 1957 my brother had left home and my father developed lung cancer. On the days when he felt very weak he asked me to drive to the outskirts of town where he took over. At the same time the mechanical maintenance of the family car became my responsibility.' Since then Phillip has had a fascination with cars and driving.

The Swanepoel smallholding was sold following the death of Phillip's father, and mother and son moved to Krugersdrop. It was there one day in February 1959 that Phillip came home from swimming and told his mother that he was feeling ill. She summoned a doctor who after a quick examination declared that Phillip was suffering either from polio or meningitis and arranged for him to be admitted to the Johannesburg Fever Hospital where he was placed in an iron lung.

The claustrophobia associated with the coffin-like breathing apparatus was such that Phillip begged to be taken out of it but the doctors replied that he would not be able to breathe outside the 'lung'. Nevertheless, he continued to plead so strongly that they finally agreed that if he could breathe on his own for a period of three hours he would be allowed to lie in a normal bed with a respirator attached to his chest. He was lifted out with nurses standing by to rush him back if the experiment failed.

Despite their anxiety Phillip survived for twice the stipulated time on his own. After that he managed to breathe independently for longer and longer periods until the chest respirator was no longer required. But with this success came the realization that the other effect of the disease was to paralyse his remaining arm.

Years later Phillip's wife Cornelia said, 'I like to think of it this way; God knew of Phillip's impatience and quick temperedness. The loss of one arm first was a trial-run to see whether he would be able to cope armless.'

Thanks to his 'impatience' Phillip made the most possible use of his legs and feet which had not been affected by his illness. After being fitted with a brace to support his head, which was unsteady due to the weakness of his neck, he was able to walk about the hospital though he had a problem of being off-balance with his single limp arm.

Despite his difficulties it was not long before he could use his foot to open a door and even play cards with his fellow patients. His real challenge came six months later when he was discharged from hospital and went home where his mother tended to his needs such as getting dressed.

Suddenly he was no longer in a situation where disability was the norm, he was alone in the world of the able-bodied which made him terribly aware of being handicapped.

'This was a bad time for me,' Phillip remembers. 'I could not go back to school and the only way I could read was to sit on the floor and turn the pages with my toes. I missed my father deeply but my sister Joey was always there to give moral support. Financially we had never had much before but now things were worse. My mother, who was not healthy herself, had received little from the sale of the smallholding and only had a small pension. I started questioning my fate and my religious faith was tested to the utmost.

'I felt very sorry for myself. What could a person without the use of their hands do? In those days many disabled people were regarded as an embarrassment and often hidden away by their families. And yet the fact that my family surrounded me with love and encouragement did very little to pull me out of my despair. I realize now it was not only a bad time for me; everybody around me was affected. I must have been a pain to the others.'

When this disheartening year ended Phillip was enrolled in Johannesburg's Hopes Home School, a special boarding school for handicapped children. Here he once more was able to feel an affinity with his disabled peers, he made friends and fun came back into his life. One problem that he had to face was that he was the school's first pupil without the use of his hands, and it was decided that he might be able to operate a typewriter by using a piece of dowel attached to a plastic mouthpiece. The Olivetti company provided the school with an electric machine and thus Phillip was able to copy class notes.

A significant point came in his life in October 1960 when the school's principal took him to the first exhibition of paintings mounted by the Association of Mouth and Foot Painting Artists in South Africa. It was there that Erich Stegmann, the Association's founder, was introduced and when he did a demonstration of mouth painting, Phillip was astonished at the speed with which he produced a portrait of one of the guests. The next day Erich visited Phillip's school and a teacher suggested that Phillip might try painting using his technique. So while Erich watched he attempted a portrait with a mouth-held brush – and achieved a circle with three dots in it for eyes and a mouth. The image was childishly simple but to the boy it was a revelation

Looking back to that significant time Phillip says, 'Mr Stegmann became my role model. My aim was to do things the way he did. It was not easy but each little thing accomplished was a great personal victory to me.'

As well as drawing with a mouth-held pencil Phillip experimented in using his toes to guide his pencil or brush and in this he became so proficient that he became one of those rare disabled painters able to produce artwork by either method.

By the beginning of 1964 Phillip's studies were completed and he returned to his mother's home and again he found that life there could be difficult.

'Sometimes I felt very frustrated when my mother was busy and I needed her to do something for me,' he explains. 'I realize now how very wise she was. By not helping me, she actually forced me to do things for myself. Remembering Erich Stegmann, I sketched a lot.'

The following year some of Phillip's pictures were sent to be evaluated at the Association's head office in Liechtenstein with the result he was accepted as a student.

What Phillip describes as 'a new and purposeful life' began when he received his MFPA grant to pay for art lessons and professional art materials. Using any odd pieces of paper with an old pencil or crayon to make his pictures became a thing of the past, and twice a week he travelled to Johannesburg to go to art classes.

'I drove myself harder and harder to learn as much as I possibly could,' says Phillip looking back on those exciting if exhausting days. 'I literally painted day and night and enjoyed every moment of it. Life had real meaning for me once more. After two years, on the first day of October 1967, I was granted full membership of the Association. I have been thanking God for Erich Stegmann ever since. Through his unselfishness I could have a new and wonderful life, and dignity with it. And I know now without any doubt in my mind that God gave me a talent for painting when I needed it most.'

Phillip's old love for cars returned after he became a professional artist, and with his mouth-held pencil he drew up plans showing how a car could be converted to be driven by a driver who had lost his hands. Helped by a friend named Cees Luyk, who was in the motor engineering business, Phillip converted a second-hand car and duly applied for a licence.

Because the request was so unusual, the test was not only conducted by a provincial traffic chief and his assistant, but also by a doctor and an engineer. Phillip and his car were put through their paces for three hours in the grounds of a driving school with half the local population looking on. At the end of the test Phillip had qualified for a learner's licence. Two weeks later he underwent a similar test which took three-and-a-half hours during which he did not make a single mistake. Phillip was then awarded what he calls his 'licence to independence'. This meant that now he was able to drive great distances in search of landscapes to paint.

Another breakthrough came in 1970 when a director of Afrikaans Films offered Phillip a part in a film.

'It told the story of a handful of mentally disturbed people and their life together in a private institution,' he explains. 'I played the role of a physically disturbed person who was hidden away from the public eye in this asylum so as not to embarrass his rich parents. It was very challenging, especially as I was acting with some of the most able actors in South Africa. The money I earned from my work in this film enabled me to buy a house so that for the first time Mother and I could move out of rented accommodation.'

PHILLIP SWANEPOEL

JOSÉ GERARDO URIBE

192

Soon-Yi Oh
White Magnolias

Soon-Yi Oh
Flowers in Winter

Professor Manuel Parreño Stone House

Professor Manuel Parreño Boats

Overleaf:
Professor Manuel Parreño
Spanish Landscape

Professor Manuel Parreño
Village Street

Professor Manuel Parreño Still Life

Elias Raftopoulos Taverna Helona

Elias Raftopoulos Island View

Elias Raftopoulos
Still Life with Flowers

Elias Raftopoulos Dancing Girls

Mai Ryan Autumn

Mai Ryan By the Shore

Grant Sharman On the Beach

Grant Sharman In the Harbour

Grant Sharman Sailing

Phillip Swanepoel   Birds on a Lake

Overleaf:
Phillip Swanepoel
African Landscape

Phillip Swanepoel   Floral Abundance

Phillip Swanepoel   Springboks

Phillip Swanepoel   African Village

José Gerardo Uribe   Landscape of Calderones, Mexico

José Gerardo Uribe   Mountain Landscape